Level
G

To the Student

This book contains exciting articles for you to read and enjoy. They tell about real-life adventures, unusual animals, famous people, interesting places, and important events.

There are questions after each article to help you think about and remember what you have read. The last question will give you a chance to write about the topic of the article.

Comprehension means "understanding." Good readers comprehend what they read. You can become a better reader and writer as you go through this book and focus on understanding.

Credits

Editorial Development: Matt Baker, Beth Spencer

Editorial Support: Joyce Ober, Anthony Moore

Cover and Interior Design: Joan Herring

Illustrators: Pages 4, 5; 8, 9; 28, 29; 46, 47; 58, 59; 74, 75; 86, 87; 94, 95 Margaret Lindmark; Pages 22, 23 Rob Williams

Photo Credits: Front cover: *Bald eagle, saguaro cactus, giraffes:* www.photos.com; *clownfish:* www.istockphoto.com/redtwiggy; *Mt. Rushmore:* www.istockphoto.com/megasquib; *open book:* www.istockphoto.com/mstay; Pages 6, 7: NASA; Pages 10, 11: www.wikipedia.org; Pages 12, 13: www.istockphoto.com/Akivi; Pages 14, 15: www.photos.com; Pages 16, 17: www.istockphoto.com/gmnicholas; Pages 18, 19: www.wikipedia.org; Pages 20, 21: www.wikipedia.org; Pages 24, 25: www.istockphoto.com/jamesbenet; Pages 26, 27: www.wikipedia.org; Pages 30, 31: www.wikipedia.org; Pages 32, 33: www.wikipedia.org; Pages 34, 35: www.wikipedia.org; Pages 36, 37: The Field Museum, #GN89671_53c; Pages 40, 41: www.wikipedia.org; Pages 42, 43: www.wikipedia.org; Pages 44, 45: www.istockphoto.com/woodstock; Pages 48, 49: www.photos.com; Pages 52, 53: www.istockphoto.com/gprentice; www.istockphoto.com/keeweebox; Pages 56, 57: www.istockphoto.com/Pete Will; Pages 62, 63: www.photos.com; Pages 64, 65: www.photos.com; Pages 66, 67: www.istockphoto.com/glubsch; Pages 68, 69: www.photos.com; Pages 70, 71: www.istockphoto.com/joeygil; Pages 72, 73: www.photos.com; Pages 76, 77: www.photos.com; Pages 78, 79: www. wikipedia.org; Pages 80, 81: www.istockphoto.com/JBolliger; Pages 82, 83: Library of Congress Prints and Photographs Division, HABS PA, 51-PHILA, 391-4; Pages 84, 85: www.photos.com; Pages 88, 89: www.photos.com; Pages 90, 91: Library of Congress Prints and Photographs Division, LC-GLB23-0575 DLC; Pages 92, 93: www.istockphoto.com/camptown

ISBN 978-0-8454-1686-0

Contents

What is the truth about pirates?

1 In movies and books, pirates sail the seas under a skull-and-crossbones flag. They carry treasure maps, wear earrings, and often have hooks or wooden pegs in place of hands or feet. Of course, these pirates are not real. Real pirates are frightening and certainly not as much fun.

2 There may have been pirates for as long as there have been ships. The first pirates existed at least 3,000 years ago. The most famous pirates, though, sailed the Caribbean Sea around 300 years ago. They included figures whose names are still well known, such as Blackbeard, Captain Kidd, and Captain Morgan. Most of today's pirate stories are based on them.

3 According to legend, pirates were free spirits who shared what they took. Historians do not agree about whether or not that is true. Most of them were dangerous criminals. They robbed and murdered innocent people on other ships and in coastal cities and towns. At that time, many were also *privateers.* Privateers were similar to pirates, but were hired by countries to attack their rivals. One of the best known privateers was Sir Francis Drake. Drake was the first Englishman to sail around the world, and he launched several daring attacks on the Spanish.

4 While they do not look much like the ones in movies, pirates still exist today. Most are in the China Sea or along the coast of Africa. They have attacked cruise ships and even stolen an oil tanker. Mostly, they operate in places where there is no Coast Guard to protect ships. Most use guns and missiles instead of swords and cannonballs. These modern-day criminals are a far cry from the legendary pirates of old.

Circle the correct answer for questions 1–5.
Write your answer to question 6 on a separate piece of paper.

1. The article does *not* say that _____.
   A pirates exist today
   B privateers are part of the Coast Guard
   C Blackbeard was alive around 300 years ago
   D there have been pirates for thousands of years

2. Which word in paragraph 3 means "enemies"?
   A rivals
   B spirits
   C pirates
   D criminals

3. Which paragraph tells about the most famous pirates?
   A 1
   B 2
   C 3
   D 4

4. You can conclude from the article that _____.
   A today's pirates still carry treasure maps
   B movies do not always show the truth
   C Captain Hook lived 300 years ago
   D pirates do not really exist

5. *Operate* can have the following meanings. Mark the meaning used in paragraph 4.
   A perform surgery
   B drive
   C work
   D use

6. Why do you think that people seem to like pirates even though they do bad things? Do you think that it's similar to the way people feel about gangsters in television and movies?

Is Pluto really a planet?

1 Most people have been taught that there are nine planets in the solar system. A growing number of scientists are not so sure about this, though. They say that Pluto, the planet farthest from the sun, is not a planet at all.

2 These scientists argue that Pluto is simply too small to be a planet. It is less than half the size of the next smallest planet, Mercury. For that matter, a number of planets have moons that are larger than Pluto, including Earth. Also, Pluto's orbit is very different from those of other planets. In fact, for years at a time it moves closer to the sun than the next planet, Neptune. This odd orbit, along with its size, makes Pluto appear more like an asteroid than a planet.

3 Other scientists say that people have been right about Pluto all along. While it may be small for a planet, it is very large compared to other asteroids. Like other planets, it has its own atmosphere. That is, it is not just a rock in space, but it is surrounded by gases. The gases that surround Earth, for instance, make up the air that people breathe. Also, like Earth and other planets, Pluto has polar ice caps. Finally, these scientists say that while Pluto's orbit may be strange, that has nothing to do with whether or not it is a planet.

4 Part of the problem is that no one agrees about the definition of a planet. There are a lot of objects circling the sun. Some are planets and some are not. For now, Pluto seems to be stuck somewhere between the definitions.

Circle the correct answer for questions 1–5.
Write your answer to question 6 on a separate piece of paper.

1. Pluto is different from other planets because it _____.
   A has an atmosphere
   B has polar ice caps
   C is much smaller
   D orbits the sun

2. Which word in paragraph 2 means "unlike in nature, form, or quality"?
   A different
   B argue
   C orbit
   D odd

3. Which paragraph tells about Pluto's atmosphere?
   A 1
   B 2
   C 3
   D 4

4. What is the main idea of the article?
   A Pluto is large compared to other asteroids.
   B No one agrees about the definition of a planet.
   C Although Pluto is considered a planet, it is really an asteroid.
   D Although Pluto is a planet, it has characteristics of both a planet and an asteroid.

5. You can conclude from the article that _____.
   A not everything that orbits the sun is a planet
   B asteroids are larger than planets
   C people can breathe on Pluto
   D Neptune is a moon

6. Write a letter to a scientist at a local university to convince him that Pluto should be considered a planet. Use facts from the article to support your position.

Where can you see four centuries of America?

1   Richmond Town is New York City's only historic village. Its buildings cover four centuries of American life. Located in La Tourette Park on Staten Island, the village first opened in 1935. In the years since, more than 15 buildings have been carefully restored on 100 acres. Several buildings still stand on their original sites. Walking through Richmond Town, you can see how a village grew and changed over more than 300 years.

2   In the 1690s, Richmond was a small village. It became Staten Island's county seat in 1728. All the government offices were there. During the American Revolution, the British took over the town. After the war, and all through the 19th century, Richmond grew. Finally, in 1898, Staten Island became part of New York City. The government offices moved away. Richmond slowly turned into a quiet neighborhood of stately homes.

3   In Richmond Town today, people dress in clothes from each historic period. They show how Staten Islanders used to do the day's activities. There are carpenters, quilters, and weavers. You can watch printing on an old press and cooking over an open fire. You can even see a 17th-century school. Voorlezer's House, built around 1695, is the oldest elementary school in the United States. There are also a one-room general store, county courthouse, churches, farmhouses, barn, shops, and a jail. Each place has furniture, toys, wagons, clothing, and other artifacts from its time period.

4   New York City is one of the busiest and most modern cities in the world. So it's good to know there's a place where people can stop and catch their breath. And while doing so, they can walk through four centuries of our country's past.

Circle the correct answer for questions 1–5.
Write your answer to question 6 on a separate piece of paper.

1. Voorlezer's House is the oldest _____ in the United States.
   A elementary school
   B furniture shop
   C farm
   D jail

2. Which word in paragraph 1 means "renewed, or brought back"?
   A opened
   B located
   C restored
   D changed

3. Which paragraph tells what happened to Richmond in the American Revolution?
   A 1
   B 2
   C 3
   D 4

4. What happened last in the history of Richmond Town?
   A Voorlezer's House was built.
   B The village opened to tourists.
   C The British took over the town.
   D It became Staten Island's county seat.

5. You can infer from the article that _____.
   A Staten Island did not want to become part of New York City
   B the British stayed in town after the American Revolution
   C schools were the same 300 years ago as now
   D a county seat is like a capital city

6. Write a paragraph for a travel brochure to convince people to visit Richmond Town. Explain why this historic village is an important attraction for all Americans.

When can one tree become a whole forest?

1   Thick rain forests cover much of South Asia. They are made up of many different kinds of trees. Sometimes as many as 179 species grow in less than three acres. All these trees live and grow close together. They share the light and the nutrients in the soil. But one tree can upset this balance. Once it gets a start in the forest, it becomes a leafy "killer." That tree is the banyan.

2   No other tree in the world grows quite like the banyan. The tree needs the help of birds to start, but it does the rest by itself. Birds drop seeds from the banyan into the upper branches of other trees in the rain forest. There the seeds sprout. New banyan branches develop from the sprouts and begin to grow.

3   As the banyan branches grow, they send roots down toward the ground. When the roots take hold in the soil, the parts above the ground grow bigger. They become new trunks from which more branches develop to send new roots down. Soon the tree that gave life to the banyan dies. It has been strangled by the new trunks and roots.

4   Meanwhile, the banyan continues to spread. New branches send down more roots which will become more new trunks. The largest banyan tree ever "counted" was in Sri Lanka, off the coast of India. It had 350 large trunks and more than 3,000 smaller ones! So it's easy to see how just one tree can look like a whole forest.

Circle the correct answer for questions 1–5.
Write your answer to question 6 on a separate piece of paper.

1. Banyan seeds are spread by _____.
    A bees
    B birds
    C wind
    D water

2. Which word in paragraph 1 means "food necessary for growth"?
    A acres
    B species
    C balance
    D nutrients

3. Which paragraph tells how many kinds of trees can grow in just a small part of a rainforest?
    A 1
    B 2
    C 3
    D 4

4. What happens last in the formation of a banyan tree?
    A Banyan parts grow bigger and become new trunks.
    B Banyan branches send roots toward the ground.
    C Banyan branches develop from sprouts.
    D Banyan roots take hold in the soil.

5. You can conclude from the article that _____.
    A banyans are popular in greenhouses
    B trees are spread out in the rain forest
    C it takes a long time to count a banyan
    D banyans don't need help from other trees to grow

6. Write a one- or two-paragraph summary of the article you just read.

1 It was a freezing winter in England. There were power outages all over the country. People sat in their cold homes and shivered. Yet inside a round, straw hut, ten people didn't mind the weather. Their blazing fire and "blankets" of animal hides kept them warm and toasty.

2 As an experiment, the group was living as people did 2,300 years ago in the Iron Age. For a whole year, the men and women went without modern things. Their car was a simple wooden cart. They washed their hair with clay. The sun was their clock. When they needed something, they had to find, grow, or make it.

3 The first three months were spent building the 48-foot round house by hand. Poles, sticks, and branches were woven together for the walls. These were coated with a mix of mud and animal hair. Finally, bundles of straw were lashed to a frame to make a thatched roof. Housing for the animals was built in the same way.

4 Providing enough food and clothing for everyone was a full-time job. Meat, milk, and eggs came from the farm animals. For other food, the group planted fields of grain. Wool from sheep made rough, but warm, dresses and shirts. Leather came from the hides of animals killed for meat. It was tied to pieces of wood to make strong shoes.

5 The people in the experiment often missed things like telephones and chocolate cake. Yet they all liked the slow, simple life of the Iron Age. They found that they could get along without the outside world when they learned to depend on one another.

Circle the correct answer for questions 1–5.
Write your answer to question 6 on a separate piece of paper.

1. The article does *not* tell _____.
   A how long it took to build the round house
   B whether there were children in the group
   C how big the round house was
   D how the people made shoes

2. Which word in paragraph 3 means "tied"?
   A spent
   B coated
   C woven
   D lashed

3. Which paragraph tells how the people got their food?
   A 1
   B 2
   C 3
   D 4

4. You can conclude from the article that people in the experiment _____.
   A could travel quickly
   B shared things like a family
   C were opposed to killing animals
   D would never live this way again

5. *Hides* can have the following meanings. Mark the meaning used in paragraph 4.
   A keeps secret
   B units of land
   C keeps out of sight
   D large, heavy skins

6. Imagine that you could travel back to another time period in history. Write a story—with you as the main character—about what daily life would be like and what adventures you might encounter.

Are all big cats alike?

1   At first sight, the cheetah and the leopard look alike. Both big cats have light tan coats, black spots, and ringed tails. If you look more carefully, though, you will see that their markings are quite different. Black stripes curve from the cheetah's eyes to its mouth like paths made by tears. The cheetah's coat also has scattered spots while the leopard's spots are clustered. The size and shape of each cat are different as well. The slimmer cheetah stands a foot taller than the leopard. But its tail is shorter, and its head is smaller. The cats also have different kinds of claws. The cheetah's are blunt and cannot be pulled in. The leopard's are sharp and retractable.

2   Both animals eat meat and are able hunters. But their ways of hunting are very different. The sleek cheetah races after its prey. It quickly reaches a top speed of 70 miles an hour, but it can't keep up this pace for long. So the cheetah must catch its prey right away or give up. The leopard, on the other hand, lies in wait, taking a rushing leap at its prey. It may even pounce on passing animals from a tree branch. Leopards are also much stronger than cheetahs. They can carry prey weighing 150 pounds 20 feet up into a tree.

3   The two cats do not act alike, either. Since they aren't as fierce as leopards, cheetahs can be tamed. Some have even been trained to hunt other animals for their masters.

4   Cheetahs and leopards do have one thing in common. Their highly prized fur has made them favorite targets for hunters. These beautiful animals are now protected by law. Perhaps this will give them a better chance for survival.

Circle the correct answer for questions 1–5.
Write your answer to question 6 on a separate piece of paper.

1. Cheetahs are _____ than leopards.
   A taller
   B meaner
   C stronger
   D better climbers

2. Which word in paragraph 1 means "able to be pulled in"?
   A alike
   B ringed
   C scattered
   D retractable

3. Which paragraph tells how leopards hunt?
   A 1
   B 2
   C 3
   D 4

4. What is the main idea of the article?
   A Cheetahs and leopards are favorite targets for hunters.
   B Cheetahs and leopards have different ways of hunting.
   C Although the cheetah and leopard do not act alike, they both eat meat.
   D Although the cheetah and leopard look alike at first sight, they are different in many ways.

5. You can infer from the article that leopards and cheetahs _____.
   A will die out if people keep hunting them
   B are better hunters than lions and tigers
   C hunt for food in the same way
   D breed together in nature

6. What other animals can you think of that look alike at first but are really very different? Describe the animals and give details on their similarities and differences.

1   On the morning of November 4, 1922, Howard Carter stepped from his house on the banks of the Nile River in Egypt. As Carter neared the spot where his men were working, he knew something had happened. All work had stopped. The men were staring into a hole they had just dug. Inside was a stone step. With growing excitement, Carter had the workers clear away the remaining steps. The final one led to a sealed wooden door.

2   Carter waited for Lord Carnarvon to join him. For nearly 16 years, the two men had searched for the tomb of an Egyptian king. Discouraged, they had agreed to give up after this year. Now, perhaps, their search had ended.

3   Hands shaking, Carter made a slit in the door. He lifted a lighted candle and peeked inside. At first he saw nothing. Then he gasped in amazement. Everywhere was the glint of gold!

4   Carter and Carnarvon had discovered the greatest treasure ever found in Egypt. Over the years, robbers had taken treasures from other tombs. But it seemed this one had not been touched. The two men stood in the tomb of the boy-king, Tutankhamen. King Tut had died more than 3,000 years before. Egyptians believed then that people went to live in another world at death. There they would need things they had used in life. King Tut had been buried with furniture, jewelry, weapons, and works of art. Many of these, like the innermost of his three coffins and his mask, were made of solid gold.

5   King Tut didn't have an easy life, though. After ruling for just ten years, he was most probably murdered by a general who wanted to be king. Today, his tomb is in the Egyptian Museum in Cairo. There, King Tut sleeps peacefully among his treasures.

Reading for Comprehension

Circle the correct answer for questions 1–5.
Write your answer to question 6 on a separate piece of paper.

1. Tutankhamen's tomb was an important discovery because _____.
   A none of its treasures had been stolen
   B no one had ever heard of that king
   C the king had ruled a long time
   D it kept Carter's crew working

2. Which word in paragraph 1 means "tightly closed"?
   A wooden
   B neared
   C stepped
   D sealed

3. Which paragraph tells how Carter and Carnarvon felt before they found the tomb?
   A 1
   B 2
   C 3
   D 4

4. Ancient Egyptians filled tombs with treasures because they _____.
   A wanted to keep things safe from robbers
   B did not consider gold to be valuable
   C had no other place to put things
   D believed in life after death

5. *Banks* can have the following meanings. Mark the meaning used in paragraph 1.
   A objects in a row
   B businesses where money is kept
   C ground along the edges of a river
   D mounds raised above the surrounding level

6. It is not known for certain how King Tut died. Come up with your own theory and write a short story about how he died and how he was buried.

Why does the aye-aye go tap-tap for food?

1 Madagascar lies off the east coast of Africa in the Indian Ocean. It is the fourth largest island in the world. About 165 million years ago, Madagascar broke away from the African continent. At that time, the same animals lived on the island and on the mainland. But over the years, the animals in each place adapted to their own special environments.

2 Take the aye-aye, for example. The aye-aye is a lemur. Lemurs are primates, cousins of monkeys and apes. The aye-aye is about the size of a squirrel and covered with brown fur. It has very large eyes and ears. Like many other lemurs, the aye-aye is busiest at night. During the day, it sleeps in its nest of twigs in a tree in the forest.

3 When night comes, the aye-aye sets off to find food. It looks for insects that have tunneled into tree trunks. To find them, the aye-aye has developed a long, thin middle finger. It uses this finger to tap the trunks. When its keen ears detect a hollow sound, the aye-aye begins to chew through the bark. Then its middle finger becomes a spoon. The aye-aye reaches through the wood to scoop out the insects. It is the only primate known to get its food in this way.

4 Like many other animals on Madagascar, and throughout the world, the aye-aye is endangered. Its forest homes are being cut down to provide land for a growing population. But luckily, this friendly little animal is protected. And aye-ayes born in zoos are now being returned to the wild.

Circle the correct answer for questions 1–5.
Write your answer to question 6 on a separate piece of paper.

1. Aye-ayes _____.
   A are found only on the African continent
   B use their sense of smell to find food
   C are related to monkeys and apes
   D hunt for food during the day

2. Which word in paragraph 4 means "threatened, or put at risk of dying out"?
   A endangered
   B protected
   C returned
   D cut

3. Which paragraph tells how the aye-aye gets its food?
   A 1
   B 2
   C 3
   D 4

4. Why are aye-ayes born in zoos being returned to the wild?
   A They can control the insect population.
   B Monkeys need to breed with them.
   C Madagascar needs more animals.
   D They are an endangered species.

5. You can infer from the article that _____.
   A lemurs are good swimmers
   B aye-ayes are large primates
   C Madagascar has many unique animals
   D aye-ayes can be seen in most American zoos

6. In poor countries like Madagascar, trying to meet the needs of people often leads to loss of animal habitat. What do you think can be done so that the needs of both people and animals are satisfied? Are there examples of this in the United States?

Who was the Red Baron?

1   In the *Peanuts* cartoon, Snoopy the dog imagines he is a World War I flying ace chasing the Red Baron. Did you ever wonder if the Red Baron might be a real person?

2   Manfred von Richthofen was the most famous pilot in the German Air Service. He loved to take chances. Born into a wealthy family, he enjoyed riding horses and hunting. When World War I started, von Richthofen was in the cavalry. He soon tired of scouting for the army and asked to join the Air Service.

3   Von Richthofen quickly learned to pilot a plane. He used his skill as a hunter to hunt enemy planes. Before long, he was shooting down more Allied planes than any other German pilot. He became a hero to the Germans. The French called him "Red Devil." But it was the British who named him the "Red Baron." Von Richthofen even painted his plane bright red. That way, everyone would immediately recognize him.

4   By 1918, the Red Baron was almost a legend in Germany. Military leaders wanted him to retire. They were afraid that if he were shot down, Germans would lose their will to fight. The Red Baron refused, saying he wouldn't stop until there were no more Germans fighting in the trenches. But he, too, was tired of war. He had shot down 80 planes, more than any pilot on either side. Yet, now he felt sad for those he had killed.

5   On April 21, 1918, not long before the war ended, von Richthofen was shot down over France. A British pilot flew over a German airfield and dropped a note telling the Germans that the Red Baron was dead. Out of respect, he was buried with full military honors in France.

Circle the correct answer for questions 1–5.
Write your answer to question 6 on a separate piece of paper.

1. Manfred von Richthofen was shot down over _____.
   A Germany
   B England
   C France
   D Russia

2. Which word in paragraph 2 means "a part of an army that is mounted on horses"?
   A pilot
   B cavalry
   C chances
   D scouting

3. Which paragraph tells how the Red Baron got his nickname?
   A 1
   B 2
   C 3
   D 4

4. Why did the Red Baron join the German Air Service?
   A He was an experienced pilot.
   B He was asked to leave the cavalry.
   C He was recruited by military leaders.
   D He was tired of scouting for the army.

5. You can conclude from the article that _____.
   A pilots in World War I flew alone
   B Germans were afraid of the Red Baron
   C the Red Baron was a hero to Americans
   D other countries had no respect for the Red Baron

6. The article says that German leaders believed the country's people would lose their will to fight if the Red Baron were shot down during World War I. Explain why you think this is so. What qualities of the Red Baron probably were most admired by the Germans?

What makes the anglerfish so interesting?

1 The anglerfish swims very slowly. So it has developed a special way to catch its food. Like people, this fish uses a fishing pole and bait. The first spine in one of the anglerfish's fins is very long. It's so long that it hangs over the fish's face like a fishing pole. A bulb at the end of the spine looks very much like bait. Some anglerfish can even wiggle this lure. When a smaller fish comes to taste the bait, the anglerfish eats it.

2 There are many kinds of anglerfish. Some live in shallow water where their lures are easy to see. Others live in the dark depths of the sea. These anglerfish have developed lures that shine through the water. The lights can even be turned off and on!

3 Yet all this is only true of female anglerfish. The males are quite different. They have no fishing poles or lures. As a matter of fact, they must count on the females for life itself. Shortly after a male hatches, it sinks its jaws into a female's body. Soon the male's mouth changes. The male becomes forever attached to the female. Even their bloodstreams are joined. If the male and female didn't come together like this, they might never find each other in the deep, dark sea.

4 In order to survive, plants and animals must often adapt their looks and the way they act. Nature's changes are not always as strange as those of the anglerfish. But the anglerfish's special features let it live where most other fish would die.

Circle the correct answer for questions 1–5.
Write your answer to question 6 on a separate piece of paper.

1. The anglerfish _____.
   A seldom eats
   B moves very slowly
   C has many sharp spines
   D lives only in lakes and streams

2. Which word in paragraph 2 means "places far below the surface in a body of water"?
   A lures
   B lights
   C kinds
   D depths

3. Which paragraph tells about the male anglerfish?
   A 1
   B 2
   C 3
   D 4

4. What does *not* happen in the life of a male anglerfish?
   A Its mouth changes.
   B It grows a long spine.
   C Its jaws sink into a female's body.
   D It joins bloodstreams with a female.

5. You can conclude from the article that _____.
   A anglerfish have broad heads
   B some other deep-sea fish glow
   C when a female anglerfish dies, its mate dies, too
   D anglerfish cannot adapt to different environments

6. People, as well as animals, have had to change in order to survive. What happens when people who have spent their whole lives in the country move to the city? When people move from the coast to the desert? Choose an example and tell what people have to do to adapt.

What were the first video games?

1   For kids today, it may seem as if there have always been video games. Many adults, on the other hand, will say that the first video games were the ones that they played as kids. Games like *PONG* and *Asteroids* were very simple, involving little more than tiny lines moving around on a black or gray screen. Still, these games were very popular in the late 1970s.

2   The truth is that video games were around long before *PONG*. In 1952, a man named A. S. Douglas created the first computer game. It was based on Tic-Tac-Toe. Then, in 1958, the first real video game was made by William Higinbotham. This game was called *Tennis for Two*. It was played on an *oscilloscope,* a device similar to a black-and-white television set with a very small, round screen.

3   *Tennis for Two* did not look much like the video sports that people play now. There were no cartoon people on the screen and no sound effects. Instead, all you saw was a gray grid with a glowing blue line at the bottom. A much smaller blue line in the middle served as a "net." With a side view of the game, players used large metal boxes to hit a glowing blue ball over the net.

4   In 1962, Steve Russell brought computer games and video games together. He invented the first video game played on a computer. Like many video games that followed, it had a science fiction theme. It was called *Spacewar!* Despite the name, though, the graphics were not much better than those of *Tennis for Two*. Without these simple games, today's video games would not exist.

Circle the correct answer for questions 1–5.
Write your answer to question 6 on a separate piece of paper.

1. The article does *not* say that _____.
   A *PONG* was the first video game
   B the graphics for *Tennis for Two* were very simple
   C William Higinbotham invented a game based on tennis
   D *Spacewar!* was the first video game played on a computer

2. Which word in paragraph 2 means "machine or tool"?
   A device
   B video
   C game
   D set

3. Which paragraph tells who built the first video game?
   A 1
   B 2
   C 3
   D 4

4. You can conclude from the article that _____.
   A A. S. Douglas built the first computer
   B early video games were all based on tennis
   C most people had oscilloscopes in their homes in 1958
   D the invention of today's video games has been a gradual process

5. *Served* can have the following meanings. Mark the meaning used in paragraph 3.
   A was used
   B provided
   C worked for
   D put the ball in play

6. If you could invent a new kind of video game, what would it be? Write a set of directions for how the game would be played.

1   In December 2004, an earthquake under the Indian Ocean caused massive flooding throughout the region. Beaches, homes, and villages were washed away in minutes. People all over the world learned the word *tsunami* (soo•NAH•mee).

2   The word *tsunami* comes from Japan. People often translate it as "tidal wave." This is not correct, though. A tsunami has little to do with the tide. Tides are caused by forces of gravity, such as the influence of the moon. A tsunami is started when an earthquake, landslide, or meteor causes a large amount of water to be *displaced*, which means pulled or pushed away from where it is. Also, it is usually a series of waves, rather than one big wave.

3   A tsunami can form due to forces from above or below. An earthquake displaces water by causing a major change in the sea floor. As the sea floor rises or falls, large waves form. Something similar occurs when there is an underwater landslide. At other times, something from above, like a meteor or landslide, causes sea water to be displaced.

4   As the tsunami moves closer to land, the ocean becomes more shallow. This causes the waves to move more slowly, but also to become taller. Their height can be up to thirty meters, or around ninety feet.

5   Fortunately, people are now working all over the world to find ways to warn people before a tsunami hits land so they can get to higher ground. There is no way to stop a tsunami from happening, but people can try to limit the damage.

Circle the correct answer for questions 1–5.
Write your answer to question 6 on a separate piece of paper.

1. A tsunami might be caused by _____.
   A high tides
   B the moon
   C a meteor
   D wind

2. Which word in paragraph 3 means "happens"?
   A occurs
   B causes
   C forces
   D displaces

3. Which paragraph gives a definition of the word *tsunami?*
   A 1
   B 2
   C 3
   D 4

4. You can conclude from the article that _____.
   A a tsunami is good for surfing
   B tsunamis are common in Japan
   C a tsunami can be very dangerous
   D no one knows how a tsunami is caused

5. *Major* can have the following meanings. Mark the meaning used in paragraph 3.
   A army officer
   B significant
   C leader
   D high

6. Imagine that you live by the ocean in an area that could be affected by a tsunami. Write a set of instructions for how you would prepare for the giant waves and what you would do if flooding occurred.

Who is Maya Angelou?

1 Maya Angelou had been a newspaper and television writer. But she had never written a book. One night, friends told Angelou that she should write her autobiography. Soon after, she began to write the story of her life. The book, *I Know Why the Caged Bird Sings,* quickly became a bestseller.

2 In the book, Angelou tells about growing up as an African American girl in the small town of Stamps, Arkansas. She and her brother lived with their grandmother in the "black" part of town. One day the grandmother took her to the only dentist in Stamps. Angelou had two badly decayed teeth. She was in terrible pain. But the white dentist refused to take care of her. He said that he did not treat African Americans. So Angelou and her grandmother traveled 25 miles to find a black dentist.

3 Angelou's writing is often about the prejudice she has felt as an African American. Her first book was published in 1970. Since then, she has written 12 more best-selling books. Six have been about herself, and three others are books of poems. In 1993, President Clinton asked Angelou to write a poem for his inauguration. Millions heard her read "On the Pulse of Morning." On that day Angelou became the first woman and first African American to speak as an American president took office.

4 But writing is only one of Angelou's talents. She speaks five foreign languages. She has acted in Broadway plays, in movies, and on television. She has written and produced other shows. In recent years she has been Professor of American Studies at Wake Forest University. She speaks to groups all over the world. Because of Maya Angelou's many talents, writing about her is like describing three or four different people.

Circle the correct answer for questions 1–5.
Write your answer to question 6 on a separate piece of paper.

1. Maya Angelou has written _____ books about herself.
   A six
   B nine
   C three
   D seven

2. Which word in paragraph 3 means "opinion formed without taking time to judge fairly"?
   A inauguration
   B published
   C prejudice
   D writing

3. Which paragraph tells about Maya's youth?
   A 1
   B 2
   C 3
   D 4

4. What happened first in the life of Maya Angelou?
   A She read a poem for President Clinton's inauguration.
   B She published her first book.
   C She wrote for a newspaper.
   D She lived in Arkansas.

5. *Treat* can have the following meanings. Mark the meaning used in paragraph 2.
   A a special snack
   B pay another's expenses
   C unexpected source of joy
   D take care of someone sick

6. Write a summary of how Maya Angelou overcame prejudice to accomplish great things.

What sticks really well without being sticky?

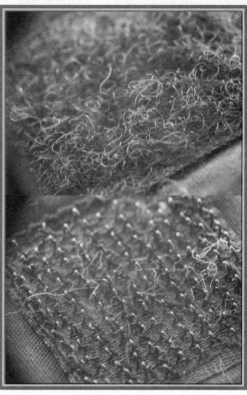

1   You may use it every time you put on your shoes. It probably fastens the shoulder pads to your sweater or jacket. It keeps a baby's diaper in place. It's used in medical supplies, automobiles, and homes. It even travels through space onboard a shuttle. What is this thing that can be used in so many different ways? And where did it come from?

2   The answer is Velcro®. Velcro takes its name from the first three letters of the words *velvet* and *crochet.* A man in Switzerland first came up with the idea. One day George deMestral returned home from a long walk in the woods. He noticed that his jacket was covered with cockleburs. As he pulled the burs from his jacket, deMestral began to wonder what made them stick so well. He decided to find out.

3   Under a microscope, deMestral could see that the bur had tiny hooks all over it. This is how the cocklebur plant spreads its seeds. The hooks stick in the fur or feathers of passing animals and birds. The animals and birds then carry the seed burs far from the "mother" plant. These hooks are also what attached themselves to the loops in the cloth of deMestral's jacket.

4   DeMestral started trying to produce these hooks and loops in a factory. He was sure that this whole new kind of fastener would have many different uses. And he was right. It has been reported that once every three days, someone somewhere comes up with a new way to use Velcro.

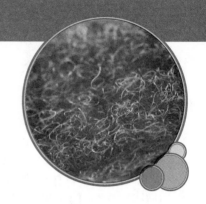

Circle the correct answer for questions 1–5.
Write your answer to question 6 on a separate piece of paper.

1. Cocklebur seeds are _____.
   A used in cooking
   B large and smooth
   C carried by the wind
   D spread by birds and animals

2. Which word in paragraph 1 means "something used to shape an article of clothing"?
   A supplies
   B sweater
   C diaper
   D pads

3. Which paragraph tells about some of the uses for Velcro?
   A 1
   B 2
   C 3
   D 4

4. What gave George deMestral the idea to invent Velcro?
   A His shoes would not stay tied.
   B His jacket was covered in cockleburs.
   C He saw birds carrying cocklebur seeds.
   D He was experimenting with hooks and loops.

5. You can infer from the article that George deMestral _____.
   A was tired of picking burs off his jacket
   B moved his factory to the United States
   C did not make much money on Velcro
   D was curious about many things

6. If you could be an inventor, what would you like to invent? Tell about your idea and how you'd go about producing it.

Where did rubber come from?

1   Spanish explorers in the New World saw Native Americans playing games with bouncing balls. The balls were made from the milky juice of a certain tree. The Spaniards called the balls "India gum" and took some back to Europe.

2   For the next 200 years, no one did much with India gum. Then an English scientist found that it rubbed out pencil marks. He began calling it "rubber." And the name stuck. So did rubber. In fact, that was the main problem in finding uses for it. In hot weather, rubber became very soft and sticky. In cold weather, it got stiff and broke apart.

3   In the early 1800s, a Scottish scientist discovered a new use for rubber. He coated two pieces of cloth with it. Then he pressed the cloths together with the rubber in the middle. It acted like a glue and made the cloth waterproof. To this day, raincoats in Great Britain are called by the scientist's name—Mackintosh.

4   Then along came an American named Goodyear. He wanted to find a way to keep rubber from getting soft and sticky or stiff and brittle. He tried mixing rubber with different chemicals. But he had no luck. Nothing seemed to make the rubber stronger until one day in 1839. That day Goodyear, by accident, spilled a mixture of rubber and chemical sulfur on a hot stove. To his surprise, the rubber stayed firm. Goodyear hung the rubber outside that night in the cold air. Sure enough, the next morning the rubber was still firm. But it was also flexible. Goodyear had discovered how to "cure" rubber so it could be used anytime and anywhere.

Circle the correct answer for questions 1–5.
Write your answer to question 6 on a separate piece of paper.

1. Rubber became _____ when it got too cold.
   A brittle
   B sticky
   C strong
   D waterproof

2. Which word in paragraph 4 means "able to bend or twist without breaking"?
   A sticky
   B flexible
   C stronger
   D chemical

3. Which paragraph tells how rubber got its name?
   A 1
   B 2
   C 3
   D 4

4. What happened first in the history of rubber?
   A Spaniards brought it to Europe.
   B A Scottish scientist coated cloth with it.
   C An American named Goodyear mixed it with sulfur.
   D An English scientist rubbed out pencil marks with it.

5. You can conclude from the article that _____.
   A Goodyear had a messy kitchen
   B British raincoats are not waterproof
   C Spanish explorers played basketball
   D sulfur helped rubber stand up to heat and cold

6. Do you think Goodyear would have discovered that the rubber and sulfur needed heat for curing without the "accident"? Why or why not?

Why did ancient Chinese bury clay armies?

1   In 1974, workers in China were digging a well near the city of Xi'an. All of a sudden their shovels hit what sounded like pottery. As they dug further, they began to find life-size clay figures. They were soldiers dressed and armed for war. The workers had accidentally discovered the tomb of China's first emperor, Qin Shi Huangdi. Shi Huangdi brought all the warring parts of China together in 221 B.C. He also ordered the building of China's Great Wall.

2   As the digging went on, huge pits were found. The largest covered about four acres. In it were 6,000 clay soldiers. What's more, they were all true to life. Each face was different. There were also pottery horses and chariots. In all, over 10,000 figures of men and horses have been found standing guard at Shi Huangdi's tomb.

3   Then in March 1990, workers were building a road about 25 miles from Shi Huangdi's tomb. They made a new discovery. Under the ground they found a network of about 24 large rooms. Inside were tens of thousands of pottery figures. It was another emperor's tomb. This one belonged to Han Jingdi. He died about 70 years after Shi Huangdi. Under Han Jingdi, the arts, science, and learning blossomed.

4   Han Jingdi's army is different from Shi Huangdi's. Like his, it is made up of soldiers, horses, and chariots. And all the faces are different. But these soldiers are painted red. They stand only about two feet high, and their wooden arms rotted away long ago. But most surprising of all is that many of the soldiers are women. Now the question is, how many more Chinese emperors' tombs are guarded by clay armies?

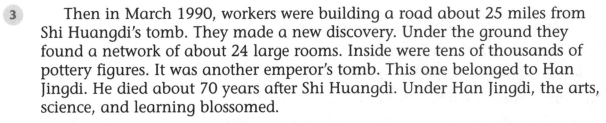

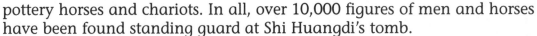

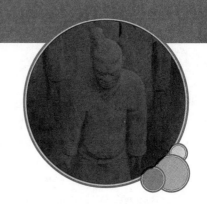

Circle the correct answer for questions 1–5.
Write your answer to question 6 on a separate piece of paper.

1. The article does *not* tell _____.

   A where the tombs are
   B when Han Jingdi died
   C when Shi Huangdi lived
   D who made the clay figures

2. Which word in paragraph 1 means "things made of clay and baked hard"?

   A pottery
   B shovels
   C figures
   D parts

3. Which paragraph compares the armies of the two emperors?

   A 1
   B 2
   C 3
   D 4

4. How was the tomb of Han Jingdi discovered?

   A Archeologists were looking for more of Shi Huangdi's tomb.
   B Archeologists had been looking for the tomb for years.
   C Workers were repairing the Great Wall of China.
   D Workers were building a road.

5. You can infer from the article that _____.

   A China's soil is mostly clay
   B China has a lot of archeologists
   C both emperors were strong rulers
   D both emperors liked the color red

6. If you could dig for historical artifacts anywhere in the world, where would you go and what would you most like to discover? Why?

1   It began on a hot summer day in 1990. Fossil hunter Sue Hendrickson was in the Badlands of South Dakota. She was helping to dig up a *Triceratops* skeleton. Her eyes kept wandering to a distant outcrop of rock. The rock had been laid down in the Cretaceous period. A few days later, Hendrickson decided to explore. She and her dog Gypsy made their way over to the outcrop.

2   Sticking out from a ledge were three large vertebrae. They looked like dinner plates. As Hendrickson looked closer, small pieces of rock tumbled down around her feet. She noticed that they were bits of bone. The bones were full of tiny holes, like a bird's. Hendrickson knew enough about dinosaurs to know that she had found something special—a very large meat eater. It turned out to be the biggest and most complete *Tyrannosaurus rex* ever discovered. The 67-million-year-old skeleton was named Sue, in honor of the woman who found her.

3   Scientists have learned a lot about *Tyrannosaurus rex* from Sue. The foot bones proved that this dinosaur was not nearly as fast as once thought. Sue probably couldn't even run. She did have a sharp sense of smell, though. The part of her brain that controlled smell was much larger than the part that controlled thought. Scientists could also tell that Sue lived a very long time—100 years or more. But they could not tell if she was cold-blooded or warm-blooded or if "she" was really "he."

4   Sue also showed that dinosaurs were closely related to birds. For example, she had a huge wishbone. Nerve pathways that led to her brain were like a bird's. And even though her leg muscles were much bigger, they, too, looked like a bird's.

5   Today, people can visit Sue in Chicago's Field Museum. Stretching 42 feet from nose to tail and standing 13 feet at the hip, this *Tyrannosaurus rex* is quite a sight.

Circle the correct answer for questions 1–5.
Write your answer to question 6 on a separate piece of paper.

1. The part of Sue's brain that controlled thought was smaller than the part that controlled _____.

   A taste
   B sight
   C smell
   D hearing

2. Which word in paragraph 1 means a "a trace of a plant or animal from a past age that has been preserved in rock"?

   A fossil
   B outcrop
   C skeleton
   D triceratops

3. Which paragraph tells how *Tyrannosaurus rex* is like a bird?

   A 1
   B 2
   C 3
   D 4

4. After Sue Hendrickson saw _____, she knew that she had found a large meat eater.

   A a wishbone
   B large vertebrae
   C an outcrop of rock
   D a *Triceratops* skeleton

5. You can infer from the article that _____.

   A Sue Hendrickson had no idea what a *Tyrannosaurus rex* looks like
   B *Tyrannosaurus rex* bones are often found in South Dakota
   C *Tyrannosaurus rex* lived during the Cretaceous period
   D Sue is a small example of *Tyrannosaurus rex*

6. Everyone seems to have a theory about how dinosaurs lived and how they died. Based on the article you just read and your own knowledge, write your ideas about the age of dinosaurs. Use as many facts as you can to back up your ideas.

1   Mary Fields was born around 1832 in a slave cabin in Tennessee. She never knew her exact birth date. As an old woman in Montana, she had a birthday whenever she felt that she needed a party. As a matter of fact, the whole town celebrated Mary's birthday!

2   Mary lived a life of adventure. Many of her experiences tied in with tall tales of the Mississippi River. For a time, Mary lived on the river. It was said that she was on the *Robert E. Lee* for its famous race against Steamboat Bill's *Natchez*. Mary looked "larger than life," too. She was over six feet tall and weighed more than 200 pounds.

3   In 1884, Mary moved west to Cascade, Montana. She went there to work at a mission. Mary was put in charge of delivering food and supplies. She spent many cold and lonely nights out on the prairie. Often she had to brave storms and wild animals to protect her supplies.

4   When she was in her 60s, Mary took a new job. She began driving a stagecoach! An old African American woman dressed in men's clothing and armed with weapons, Mary presented quite a picture. She was known for delivering people and goods on time, no matter what the weather. Her stagecoach days came to an end in 1903. But Mary decided to stay on in Cascade. She soon became the town's number one baseball fan. She gave flowers from her garden to anyone on the Cascade team who hit a home run. Stagecoach Mary died in 1914. And the people of Cascade mourned her as a true legend of the Wild West.

Circle the correct answer for questions 1–5.
Write your answer to question 6 on a separate piece of paper.

1. The article does *not* tell _____.
   A when Mary moved to Montana
   B which steamboat won the race
   C how Mary looked
   D when Mary died

2. Which word in paragraph 4 means "felt or showed sadness"?
   A armed
   B dressed
   C mourned
   D presented

3. Which paragraph tells about Mary's work at the mission?
   A 1   C 3
   B 2   D 4

4. What happened first in Mary's life?
   A She lived on the Mississippi River.
   B She moved to Cascade, Montana.
   C She began driving a stagecoach.
   D She became a baseball fan.

5. You can infer from the article that _____.
   A Mary was never on time
   B Mary was a good swimmer
   C Mary was afraid to travel by herself
   D Mary was loved by the people of Cascade

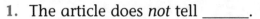

6. Throughout history, many Western characters have become legends—Wild Bill Hickok, Calamity Jane, Jim Beckwourth, and Davy Crockett to name a few. What sets these people apart from "regular people"? Write a profile of your favorite legend. It can be about a real or make-believe person. Just make sure your hero is "larger than life."

What horse is truly wild?

1   The Przewalski's (shuh•VAL•skees) horse is more like a pony in size. It stands about 13 hands high (52 inches). And it looks a little like a donkey. The Przewalski's horse has a grayish-brown coat. Its mane is dark brown and sticks straight up. Each horse is lighter in color around its mouth. There is also a dark stripe along its back and dark bars on its lower legs.

2   In fact, the Przewalski's horse is very special. It is the only true wild horse in the world today. Horses like the mustangs of the American West are called "wild." But they really are descended from tame horses that ran away. The Przewalski's horse is different. It roamed Mongolia wild and free for thousands of years. Very few have ever been tamed.

3   These horses have always shied away from people. So no one really knew about them until the 1880s. In 1881, a Russian explorer named Przewalski found the skull of a horse in central Asia. But it wasn't until 20 years later that people captured a few Przewalski's horses. The animals began to die out when people started living on their land. Their horses took water and grazing land from the wild ones.

4   Today, there are around 1,500 Przewalski's horses left. Almost all of them live in zoos or wildlife parks around the world. Scientists carefully control the animals' breeding. In this way, they hope to keep the line alive and strong. Some younger horses have been released into the wild in Mongolia. The scientists hope that from this stock new herds will grow. Then Przewalski's horses will once again thunder across the steppes of central Asia.

Circle the correct answer for questions 1–5.
Write your answer to question 6 on a separate piece of paper.

1. The article does *not* tell _____.
   A where Przewalski's horses are found today
   B when Przewalski's horses were captured
   C how Przewalski's horses were captured
   D why mustangs aren't really wild

2. Which word in paragraph 2 means "came down"?
   A called
   B tamed
   C roamed
   D descended

3. Which paragraph tells what the Przewalski's horse looks like?
   A 1
   B 2
   C 3
   D 4

4. Why did the Przewalski's horse begin to die out in the 1900s?
   A The climate in the area began to change.
   B They were taken to zoos and wildlife parks.
   C People killed them for their meats and hides.
   D People and horses started living on their land.

5. You can infer from the article that the Przewalski's horse is _____.
   A easy to ride
   B bred in zoos
   C used for racing
   D mean to people

6. Do you think Przewalski's horses should stay in zoos and wildlife parks where they will be safe? Or should they all be released to live in the wild once again? Give reasons to support your opinion.

Who really wrote Shakespeare's plays?

1   For centuries, people have enjoyed *Romeo and Juliet, Hamlet,* and many other plays by William Shakespeare. However, some people who study Shakespeare's plays say that he did not actually write them. There are many reasons why they think this.

2   One reason has to do with his education. Shakespeare left school at a young age and had very poor handwriting. Neither his father nor his daughter could write at all. So how could he be such a great writer?

3   Another argument has to do with the settings of the plays. Some of them take place in royal courts in England and other countries. Because Shakespeare was not born to a "noble" family, he could not have known what life was like in a court. So how could he have written about it?

4   One possible author of the plays is Edward de Vere. He was a well-educated aristocrat in the court of Queen Elizabeth. He wrote when he was young but then seemed to stop. Some people suspect that he kept on writing. He used "William Shakespeare" as a pen name because writing plays was not considered proper for a person of his class. Other possible authors include the famous writers Francis Bacon and Christopher Marlowe.

5   Still, most experts believe that the person who wrote the plays was Shakespeare himself. They say that he was self-taught. Although his handwriting was bad, that was also true of many other writers. Royal courts, they argue, were nothing like what is seen in the plays. That means that the person who wrote about them had not been part of them. The debate goes on.

Circle the correct answer for questions 1–5.
Write your answer to question 6 on a separate piece of paper.

1. The article says that all of the following might have written William Shakespeare's plays *except* _____.
   A Francis Bacon
   B Edward de Vere
   C Queen Elizabeth
   D William Shakespeare

2. Which word in paragraph 4 means "writer"?
   A aristocrat
   B author
   C class
   D pen

3. Which paragraph tells why people think that William Shakespeare really did write the plays?
   A 2
   B 3
   C 4
   D 5

4. You can infer from the article that _____.
   A Francis Bacon knew Queen Elizabeth
   B Shakespeare wrote *Hamlet* but not *Romeo and Juliet*
   C most experts do not believe that Shakespeare wrote the plays
   D there is still a lot that people do not know about Shakespeare

5. *Noble* can have the following meanings. Mark the meaning used in paragraph 3.
   A possessing outstanding qualities
   B of high birth or exalted rank
   C grand in appearance
   D chemically inactive

6. Give your theory on whether William Shakespeare did or did not write the plays himself. Use information from the article to support your argument.

What are the La Brea Tar Pits?

1   The La Brea Tar Pits are exactly what they sound like. During the early years of Los Angeles, people found uses for the large pools of foul-smelling, sticky black asphalt. While Native Americans in the area made canoes and baskets with the tar, more recent settlers used it for their roofs. So how did the tar pits become a tourist attraction?

2   It turned out that there were a lot of old bones in the tar. For a long time, people assumed that they came from cattle. Starting in 1901, though, scientists found that the bones came from a wide variety of creatures. Some of these were animals that still exist in the area. Many, though, came from creatures that are extinct. These included native horses, camels, and giant birds. They provide a picture of what the area looked like thousands of years ago.

3   For one thing, the area was probably a lot wetter and colder. Also, it probably was a much more dangerous place to live. One species that lived there was the *mastodon,* a huge animal like an elephant with long tusks. Another was the gray wolf. Many of the bones found in the pits, though, come from saber-toothed tigers. These creatures, as their name suggests, had long, sharp front teeth.

4   Animals fell into the tar pits over a very long period of time. For all the bones in the La Brea Tar Pits to have gotten there, a large animal would have had to have fallen in only once in 10 years over a period of 30,000 years.

Circle the correct answer for questions 1–5.
Write your answer to question 6 on a separate piece of paper.

1. The article says that bones from all the following have been found in the tar pits *except* _____.
   A saber-toothed tigers
   B mastodons
   C dinosaurs
   D camels

2. Which word in paragraph 2 means "gone from the Earth"?
   A exist
   B native
   C extinct
   D assumed

3. Which paragraph tells about what tar from the pits has been used for?
   A 1
   B 2
   C 3
   D 4

4. You can conclude from the article that _____.
   A saber-toothed tigers became extinct from falling into tar pits
   B people can learn a lot about the past from looking at bones
   C tar comes from bones
   D mastodons ate cattle

5. *Found* can have the following meanings. Mark the meaning used in paragraph 2.
   A learned
   B located
   C begin
   D pour

6. Imagine that you lived in prehistoric Los Angeles. Write a journal entry describing a day living in the world of mastodons and saber-toothed tigers.

1 Mary Cassatt always wanted to be an artist. But she didn't respect the art teachers in America or admire the pictures they painted. Cassatt decided to go to Europe. There she could study and learn from the great artists of the mid-1800s. So at the age of 21, Cassatt left Pennsylvania and moved to Paris.

2 Soon Cassatt found she didn't like her French art teacher any better than her American ones. What she really disliked were the rules of painting. She felt artists should be free to paint any way they wanted to. Cassatt began to study on her own. She traveled through Europe visiting museums. The young artist was awed by the paintings she saw and tried to copy them. Slowly, Cassatt developed her own style of painting. She began to paint what she knew best—moments in the lives of women.

3 Cassatt moved back to Paris. There she met other artists who also broke the rules. These were the Impressionists. Cassatt soon joined them. At first, people hated this new art. They didn't understand Impressionism. The artists used light, bright colors and quick, sketchy brush strokes. They wanted to give just an "impression" of real people in real settings. In time the Impressionists became very important in the world of art. And Mary Cassatt became one of the few famous women Impressionists.

Circle the correct answer for questions 1–5.
Write your answer to question 6 on a separate piece of paper.

1. Mary Cassatt is best known for painting _____.
   A landscapes
   B buildings
   C animals
   D women

2. Which word in paragraph 3 means "roughly drawn"?
   A famous
   B sketchy
   C quick
   D real

3. What happened last in the life of Mary Cassatt?
   A She began to paint moments in the lives of women.
   B She traveled through Europe visiting museums.
   C She left Pennsylvania to study in Paris.
   D She became one of the Impressionists.

4. Why did Mary Cassatt decide to study on her own?
   A She disliked the rules of painting.
   B She aspired to be an Impressionist.
   C She wanted to travel through Europe.
   D She didn't respect American art teachers.

5. You can infer from the article that _____.
   A Mary Cassatt didn't like following rules
   B Mary Cassatt liked her French art teacher
   C everyone loved Impressionism from the beginning
   D Impressionism never gained popularity outside of Paris

6. Before Impressionism, most paintings were "larger than life." They were full of symbols, such as good and evil, and important messages. Why do you think it was hard for people to accept the Impressionists?

1   Are the following statements about moose true or false? *Moose antlers and noses are eaten by people.* True. Some people eat roasted moose antlers. They even eat moose nose! First the bones are taken out. Then it is boiled in water with onions, salt, and pepper. *Moose are easily trained.* True again. Although fully grown male moose are hard to handle, many moose can be trained to pull sleighs. *Moose were once no larger than cats.* That's true, too. Like other animals in the deer family, moose were as small as cats millions of years ago.

2   Today moose are huge animals. Sometimes they grow taller than seven feet and weigh up to 1,800 pounds. They are so big that hunters have a problem getting a dead moose back to camp. Native Americans used to solve this problem very cleverly. They just moved their camp to the moose until the giant beast was completely eaten! Despite their large size, moose swim very well. They can often swim faster than a person can row a boat. They are also good at jumping. A hunter once saw a moose jump more than six feet over a fallen pine tree.

3   At one time, hunters killed nearly all the moose in the eastern United States. Then laws were passed to protect this remarkable animal. Now there are nearly half a million moose in North America. They live from Maine to Alaska. In fact, more species of moose are found in North America than anywhere else in the world.

Circle the correct answer for questions 1–5.
Write your answer to question 6 on a separate piece of paper.

1. Moose are _____.
   A hard to train
   B good swimmers
   C found only in Alaska
   D not protected from hunters

2. Which word in paragraph 2 means "find the answer to"?
   A grow
   B solve
   C moved
   D problem

3. It is likely that the moose population will remain stable because _____.
   A moose are no longer eaten
   B more moose are being used to pull sleighs
   C laws have been passed to protect the moose
   D moose are moving into other parts of the United States

4. You can infer from the article that _____.
   A cat-size moose still live in North America
   B moose are popular pets in North America
   C certain types of moose live outside North America
   D moose are no longer hunted outside North America

5. *Family* can have the following meanings. Mark the meaning used in paragraph 1.
   A a series of elements
   B a category of related animals
   C a group united by convictions
   D a group related by common characteristics

6. One of the places in North America where moose can be seen is Rocky Mountain National Park in Colorado. Write a short promotional piece for the park that explains to people why the moose is such a unique animal that must be seen.

Why did African Americans go back to Africa?

1 At the end of the Revolutionary War, there were still people in the new United States who were loyal to Great Britain. They wanted no part of our young country. Many of these people moved north to Canada. About 30,000 Loyalists settled in Nova Scotia. Among them were about 4,000 African Americans. Most were already free, but some were still slaves.

2 The British, who still ruled Canada, promised grants of land to all the Loyalists. But for many African Americans the promises never came true. There was no free land for them. Then the Sierra Leone Company in London heard about their problems. The trading company had a colony in West Africa in need of settlers. So the Sierra Leone Company said they would give free passage to any African Americans who were willing to settle in the new colony. More than 500 families agreed to begin a new life in West Africa.

3 In 1792, a fleet of 15 ships sailed from Nova Scotia. Onboard were more than 1,100 African Americans. These brave men, women, and children helped the colony in Sierra Leone to grow. They founded a new port city there, named Freetown. Today it is the capital of the nation of Sierra Leone.

4 In 1992, African Americans who still lived in Nova Scotia gathered for the bicentennial, or 200th anniversary, of the voyage to Sierra Leone. They celebrated both the families who stayed in Canada and those who went back to Africa.

Circle the correct answer for questions 1–5.
Write your answer to question 6 on a separate piece of paper.

1. The article does *not* tell _____.
   A where Sierra Leone is
   B when the Loyalists left Canada
   C what the capital of Sierra Leone is
   D how the Loyalists made a living in Sierra Leone

2. Which word in paragraph 2 means "gifts of land for a special purpose"?
   A grants
   B settlers
   C promises
   D problems

3. Which paragraph tells about the bicentennial celebration?
   A 1
   B 2
   C 3
   D 4

4. What happened after African American Loyalists arrived in Sierra Leone?
   A The Revolutionary War ended.
   B Loyalists settled in Nova Scotia.
   C The city of Freetown was founded.
   D The British offered land grants to Loyalists.

5. You can infer from the article that _____.
   A the Sierra Leone Company was part of the British government
   B not all African American Loyalists moved to Sierra Leone
   C some Loyalists worked as slaves in Sierra Leone
   D Sierra Leone is no longer a country

6. Do you think it was easy or difficult for the African Americans to go back to Africa? Why do you think so?

What creatures will you find in New Zealand?

1   The islands of New Zealand are home to many unique creatures. Left alone for millions of years, they have evolved into animals found nowhere else on Earth. So you will find there strange birds and insects, some of which no longer fly. Kiwis and wetas are two of these.

2   The kiwi is New Zealand's national bird. It's about the size of a chicken, with shaggy, brown feathers sticking out all over. The kiwi has a long, slender bill. At its end, unlike any other known bird, are two nostrils. The kiwi's nostrils "nose" out food in the forests where it lives. Instead of a tree, this shy bird's home is a hole in the ground. The kiwi comes out at night to hunt for insects and other food.

3   Another thing sets the kiwi apart from most birds. The female lays just one egg, but it's a huge one. Then she turns the care of the egg over to the male. He sits on it until it hatches. Sadly, the kiwi population is getting smaller. If care isn't taken, this strange bird may soon be found only in captivity.

4   Wetas were one of the first forms of animal life on the islands of New Zealand. And they haven't changed much in the last 200 million years. The weta may be the largest insect on Earth. Some of them grow to be about the size of a mouse. They can weigh as much as two and a half ounces.

5   Looking a bit like a cricket, the weta has long, spiny legs and a hard shell. It uses its back legs to protect itself by kicking out at anything that frightens it. The people of New Zealand are very proud of their wetas. Even if they're "only bugs," they're the biggest bugs in the world!

Circle the correct answer for questions 1–5.
Write your answer to question 6 on a separate piece of paper.

1. This article does *not* tell _____.
   A how the kiwi differs from other birds
   B where the kiwi builds its nest
   C how old the weta is
   D what the weta eats

2. Which word in paragraph 1 means "developed slowly over time"?
   A creatures
   B evolved
   C islands
   D found

3. Which paragraph tells about the size of the weta?
   A 1
   B 2
   C 3
   D 4

4. You can conclude from the article that _____.
   A certain types of kiwi can fly
   B many kiwis hatch from one egg
   C kiwis and wetas are friendly to humans
   D New Zealand takes pride in its unique creatures

5. *Bill* can have the following meanings. Mark the meaning used in paragraph 2.
   A bird's jaws with their horny covering
   B account of cost of goods or services
   C visor of a cap
   D draft of a law

6. Write a paragraph about the kiwi that can be used in a New Zealand travel brochure. Highlight the things that make it special and why people outside the country should see it.

What was America's first submarine?

1   It was the night of September 6, 1776. The American Revolution had begun. Americans were fighting for their independence from Great Britain. British ships were in New York Harbor. The Americans decided to try something new to get rid of them. Sergeant Ezra Lee was assigned the job of sinking the largest of the British ships, the *Eagle*.

2   Lee stepped into America's first war submarine, the *Turtle*. It was made of oak timbers held together by iron bands. Inside there was room for only one person. Handles in the submarine were attached to propellers and a rudder. Lee steered by cranking the propellers and moving the rudder. He brought the *Turtle* next to the British ship.

3   Then Sergeant Lee opened a pipe in the bottom of the submarine. Water filled a tank inside the *Turtle*. That let it dive under the *Eagle*. Next, Lee pushed up on an iron tube sticking out of the top of the submarine. At the end of this tube was a screw. The screw was attached by a rope to a mine. Sergeant Lee planned to twist the screw into the bottom of the *Eagle*.

4   The American tried several times to attach the mine. But a metal plate covered the bottom of the *Eagle*. The screw couldn't pierce this hard covering. Discouraged and tired, Lee headed back to shore. To move faster through the water, he decided to make the *Turtle* lighter. He dumped the 250-pound mine into the water. Soon after Sergeant Lee landed, the mine blew up. When the British heard the explosion, they were alarmed. They sailed out of the harbor. So in a way, the *Turtle* did its job. For the time being, New York City was safe from the British.

Circle the correct answer for questions 1–5.
Write your answer to question 6 on a separate piece of paper.

1. The *Turtle* was _____.
   A destroyed after Sergeant Lee's mission
   B bigger than the *Eagle*
   C made of oak timbers
   D built to carry two

2. Which word in paragraph 4 means "go through"?
   A attach
   B pierce
   C move
   D make

3. Which paragraph tells how Sergeant Lee planned to sink the British ship?
   A 1
   B 2
   C 3
   D 4

4. What drove the British ship out of New York Harbor?
   A The *Turtle's* screw damaged the ship's metal plate.
   B The captain saw the *Turtle* approaching.
   C The British crew heard an explosion.
   D A mine damaged part of the ship.

5. You can conclude from the article that the *Turtle* _____.
   A was never used again
   B had several advanced controls
   C carried cargo swiftly through the water
   D was a new idea that still needed more work

6. Suppose the *Turtle* had been able to blow up the *Eagle*. What effect do you think that would have had on the British? On the Americans? On the Revolutionary War?

Why is the "king of cactuses" in danger?

1   The giant saguaro (sa•GUA•ro) has always been a "survivor." It has had to be. This cactus grows in the deserts of Arizona, California, and Mexico. These places often get fewer than five inches of rain in a whole year. But the saguaro is perfectly suited to life in the desert. Saguaro roots are shallow and spread out about 50 feet around the plant. In this way, the cactus traps every drop of water possible.

2   Saguaros stand tall and proud in the desert. A fully grown plant may be 60 feet tall and weigh as much as 10 tons. Some plants live up to 200 years. The saguaro grows very slowly. A 10-year-old plant may be only one inch tall! The saguaro's white flowers don't bloom until it's at least 50 years old. The "arms" don't start growing until the plant reaches the age of 75.

3   Now the saguaro is menaced by more than nature. Cities of the Southwest are growing fast. They need more and more land. Saguaros and other plants are being destroyed to make way for new roads and buildings. The saguaro is also prized by people who want rare plants in their gardens. So cactus "poachers" dig up saguaros. In less than half an hour, these thieves can dig up a 90-year-old plant, put it in a truck, and drive away. Then they turn around and sell it.

4   Because the saguaro grows so slowly, each lost plant takes many years to replace. So the U.S. Fish and Wildlife Service works hard to keep people from taking or destroying saguaros. This is a fight that must be won. Only then will the giant saguaro continue to "rule" over the desert.

Circle the correct answer for questions 1–5.
Write your answer to question 6 on a separate piece of paper.

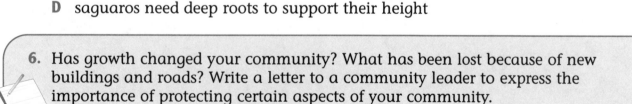

1. The saguaro _____.
   A grows in deserts of the Southwest
   B blooms when it is 10 years old
   C has bright red flowers
   D lives for 50 years

2. Which word in paragraph 3 means "threatened, or put in danger"?
   A turn
   B prized
   C menaced
   D destroyed

3. Which paragraph tells about the saguaro's size?
   A 1
   B 2
   C 3
   D 4

4. Saguaros are in danger in the Southwest mostly because _____.
   A the ground is becoming too dry
   B cactus poachers dig them up and sell them
   C land is being taken over by roads and buildings
   D the U.S. Fish and Wildlife Service doesn't protect them

5. You can infer from the article that _____.
   A saguaros are not threatened
   B it's a crime to dig up a saguaro
   C saguaros spread and grow quickly
   D saguaros need deep roots to support their height

6. Has growth changed your community? What has been lost because of new buildings and roads? Write a letter to a community leader to express the importance of protecting certain aspects of your community.

Who was Walt Disney?

1   When Walt Disney decided to move west, he was only 21 years old and very poor. He left Kansas City, Missouri, for Hollywood, California, with just a few dollars in his pocket. In Kansas City he had been in business with a friend. They had made cartoon ads for movie theaters. But the business had failed.

2   In Hollywood, Disney found a way to use his talents. Cartoon movies were in their early stage. He wanted to turn them into a new art form. He started out in 1928 with a movie about a mouse named Mortimer. Disney liked mice. In fact, while growing up on his parents' farm, he had come to like all animals. Later, Mortimer Mouse got a new name—Mickey. For more than 30 years, Disney was the voice of Mickey Mouse.

3   In 1937, Disney made his first feature-length cartoon, *Snow White and the Seven Dwarfs.* Just one minute of the story needed nearly 360 drawings. More than 700 artists worked on *Snow White* for several years. But it was one of the most popular movies ever made and won many awards.

4   Over the years, Disney had huge hits with *Pinocchio, Bambi, Peter Pan, Cinderella,* and other cartoons. He also made films about nature. But he had another dream. He wanted to build a park where children of all ages could step into a world of fantasy. Disneyland, which opened in 1955, was the answer to his dream. And before he died in 1966, Disney had made plans for Disney World. Through his movies and parks, Walt Disney brought magic to the lives of many Americans. And now with parks in other countries, this world of fantasy covers the globe.

Circle the correct answer for questions 1–5.
Write your answer to question 6 on a separate piece of paper.

1. The article does *not* tell about Walt Disney's _____.
   A career
   B school years
   C theme parks
   D first business

2. Which word in paragraph 4 means "something make-believe"?
   A fantasy
   B nature
   C globe
   D films

3. Which paragraph tells about Walt Disney's first mouse?
   A 1
   B 2
   C 3
   D 4

4. More than 700 artists worked on *Snow White* because _____.
   A they worked two-hour shifts
   B it was such a popular movie
   C it was Walt Disney's first feature-length cartoon
   D the story needed nearly 360 drawings per minute

5. You can infer from the article that _____.
   A Walt Disney was afraid of animals
   B Walt Disney worked hard for his success
   C cartoon movies are no longer being made
   D cartoon movies have always been drawn by hand

6. Over the years, Walt Disney introduced many different cartoon characters. Which is your favorite Disney character, and why?

What is quinine?

1   Have you ever heard of the disease malaria? It is spread by mosquitoes in hot, wet places such as a rain forest. It makes people very sick. They run high fevers and hurt all over. Each new attack leaves them weaker. If their fever doesn't break, they die. There is something that fights malaria, though. It is quinine (KWEYE•nine).

2   Quinine comes from the bark of the cinchona (sin•KOH•nuh). This tree grows up around 5,000 feet in the Andes Mountains of South America, from Colombia south to Bolivia. An old legend tells how quinine was discovered.

3   According to the story, a young Indian was lost in the Andes jungle. He was burning with fever and badly in need of water. Finally, he came upon a pool of still water. The Indian threw himself to the ground and began to drink. The water tasted terrible. It was very bitter. When the Indian looked around, he saw that the bark of a tree he knew as quina-quina had fallen into the water. He thought he would die from drinking the bitter water. But he was so thirsty, he didn't care. To his surprise, not only did he not die, but his fever went away. Soon the Indian was strong enough to make his way back to his village. From then on, Indians used the bark of the quina-quina tree to cure fever.

4   The first known use of quinine by Europeans was in the early 1600s. Spanish priests in Peru used it to cure malaria. Soon it was sent to Europe. Later, a European scientist gave a new name to the tree quinine came from. He called it cinchona after the wife of the Spanish ruler of Peru.

Circle the correct answer for questions 1–5.
Write your answer to question 6 on a separate piece of paper.

1. The article does *not* tell how _____.
   A Spanish priests used quinine
   B quinine is made today
   C malaria is spread
   D quinine tastes

2. Which word in paragraph 3 means "tasting sharp, not sweet"?
   A burning
   B thirsty
   C strong
   D bitter

3. Which paragraph tells about the disease malaria?
   A 1
   B 2
   C 3
   D 4

4. Spanish priests in Peru used quinine to cure malaria because _____.
   A it was known to cure fever
   B the wife of Peru's leader told them to
   C quinine already had been used in Spain
   D it tasted better than the bark of other trees

5. You can infer from the article that _____.
   A quinine only cures Indians' fevers
   B other trees in South America have quinine
   C malaria has been wiped out around the world
   D the word *quinine* comes from the Indian name for the cinchona

6. Write your own legend about how quinine was discovered. Be sure to use a different character and setting than the legend in the article.

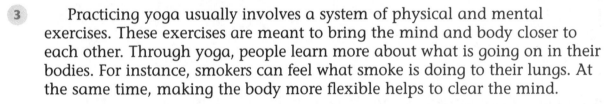

1   Not long ago, most people would give you funny looks if you said you practiced yoga. They thought it was a strange cult of people standing on their heads. Today, though, people are learning yoga everywhere. In some schools it is even taught in gym class.

2   While yoga may be new to most people in the United States, it is more than 5,000 years old. It comes from India, where the word *yoga* means "join together" in the ancient *sanskrit* language. While yoga has been tied to the Hindu religion, today it is practiced by people of any beliefs.

3   Practicing yoga usually involves a system of physical and mental exercises. These exercises are meant to bring the mind and body closer to each other. Through yoga, people learn more about what is going on in their bodies. For instance, smokers can feel what smoke is doing to their lungs. At the same time, making the body more flexible helps to clear the mind.

4   The three main parts of a yoga practice involve exercise, meditation, and breathing. The exercise part involves many different *asanas,* or poses, with names like "downward facing dog" and "full lotus." There are also head-stands that help to make the body stronger and more flexible. Meditation involves sitting quietly to clear the mind. The "breathing" part sounds very easy to most people. In yoga, however, people learn to control their breath, which can take a lot of work.

5   There are more than 100 different kinds of yoga. Some are very different from what is described here.

Circle the correct answer for questions 1–5.
Write your answer to question 6 on a separate piece of paper.

1. The article does *not* tell _____.
   A why people meditate
   B where yoga comes from
   C what the word *yoga* means
   D what the most popular form of yoga is

2. Which word in paragraph 1 means "small religious group"?
   A gym
   B cult
   C yoga
   D schools

3. Which paragraph tells how old yoga is?
   A 1
   B 2
   C 3
   D 4

4. What is *not* one of the positive effects of practicing yoga?
   A It teaches people what is going on in their bodies.
   B It makes the body stronger and more flexible.
   C It helps to clear the mind.
   D It builds muscle mass.

5. You can conclude from the article that _____.
   A yoga started in the United States
   B yoga is only practiced by Hindus
   C yoga can help people be healthier
   D yoga never involves standing on your head

6. Many people do yoga for "peace of mind." What do you like to do when you want to clear your thoughts? Describe the process you go through.

What are windmills used for?

1   Today, the place where most people see windmills is on miniature golf courses. The windmill seems to be a thing from the distant past. That may change, though. Windmills are making a comeback.

2   A windmill creates energy from wind. The way it works is that the wind moves long blades. The blades are attached to a shaft, which is connected to a machine. The machine uses the power that comes from the wind.

3   The oldest windmills are thought to have been built in Persia in the 7th century A.D. Soon they spread to China, and then to Europe. Early windmills generally had sails instead of blades. They were mostly used for milling grain or pumping water. Later, they also served a number of other purposes. These included making paper and cutting logs.

4   In Denmark in the 1890s, people came up with yet another use for the windmill. This use became very important in small towns in the United States until the 1930s. The windmill, it turned out, could be used to generate electricity. A windmill that creates electricity is called a *wind turbine generator*. A collection of wind turbines in the same location is known as a *wind farm*. The U.S. has several of the largest wind farms in the world. The largest U.S. wind farm is the Stateline Wind Energy Center on the Oregon–Washington line, producing enough electricity to power 70,000 households.

5   Windmills became less popular in the 20th century. Fossil fuels like oil were much less expensive and easier to use. Now, though, fossil fuels are becoming harder to find and more costly. Also, people are concerned about the air pollution that fossil fuels cause. Wind power does not pollute the environment, and it will never run out.

Circle the correct answer for questions 1–5.
Write your answer to question 6 on a separate piece of paper.

1. Windmills are *not* used to _____.
   A cut wood
   B sail ships
   C mill grain
   D pump water

2. Which word in paragraph 5 means "worried"?
   A pollute
   B popular
   C expensive
   D concerned

3. Which paragraph tells why windmills are becoming popular again?
   A 1
   B 2
   C 4
   D 5

4. What has *not* been a factor in windmills becoming more popular in recent years?
   A fossil fuels causing air pollution
   B fossil fuels pumping too little water
   C fossil fuels becoming harder to find
   D fossil fuels becoming more expensive

5. You can conclude from the article that _____.
   A windmills are an old way to create power that is becoming popular again
   B windmills generate electricity for miniature golf courses
   C people in 7th century Persia used a lot of electricity
   D wind is a fossil fuel

6. Write a letter to the editor of your local newspaper to convince more companies in your area to replace fossil fuels with wind turbine generators. Highlight the advantages to the companies and the community.

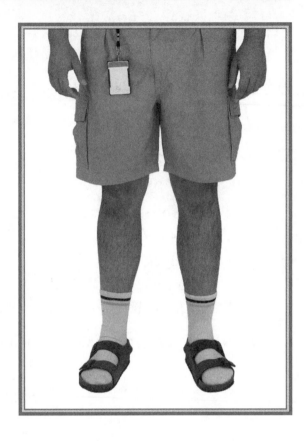

1   In 1966, Margot Fraser was making her yearly visit to Germany. Sore feet were keeping her from having fun. At a health spa in Bavaria, a trainer suggested she try a comfortable German sandal—the Birkenstock. The sandals made Margot's feet feel much better. So she decided to bring some home to sell in America. At first, she just sold Birkenstocks from her home. People who tried these strange sandals were really pleased with their comfort. Yet when Margot tried to interest shoe stores in them, people turned her down. "No woman would wear a shoe that looks like this!" they laughed.

2   Margot kept trying to build interest in her Birkenstocks. Finally, at a health food store convention in San Francisco in 1967, she found her first real customers. Now she could start her own company. But she had no business training, no plan of operation, and no credit. Margot did have one thing, though. Birkenstock in Germany had agreed to let her be the exclusive American agent for their shoes.

3   The way Margot treated people helped her succeed. She believed then—and still does—that people should be treated fairly, kindly, and with respect. Margot's company, Birkenstock Distribution USA, isn't run like a lot of companies the same size. Margot asks her workers for their ideas. And she listens to what they have to say. As a matter of fact, Margot says her success probably comes from not having any business training. Because she didn't have a lot of money at first, she had to have better ideas. Her ideas seem to have paid off. Margot Fraser has grown her company from a small home business to the multi-million dollar company it is today.

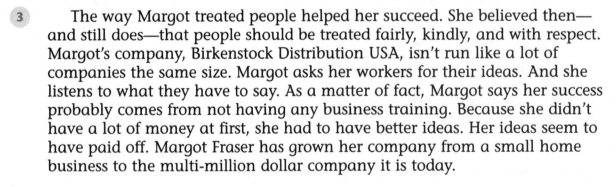

Circle the correct answer for questions 1–5.
Write your answer to question 6 on a separate piece of paper.

1. Margot Fraser visited Germany _____.
   A once a year
   B once a week
   C once a month
   D every other year

2. Which word in paragraph 2 means "single or sole; only"?
   A credit
   B agent
   C exclusive
   D convention

3. What happened last in the article?
   A Birkenstock Distribution USA became a multi-million dollar company.
   B Birkenstock agreed to let Margot be their exclusive U.S. agent.
   C Margot went to a health food store convention.
   D Margot started her own company.

4. What was most important in enabling Margot to generate more interest in her shoes and start her own company?
   A selling shoes from her home
   B writing a detailed business plan
   C bringing home sandals from Germany
   D finding customers at a health food store convention

5. You can infer from the article that _____.
   A Margot still has sore feet
   B Margot's workers enjoy their work
   C Margot no longer goes to conventions
   D Margot's company doesn't have repeat customers

6. Do you think Margot's way of running her business could work in just about any kind of company? Why or why not? Would you appreciate working for someone who had this management style?

Why are there so few mountain gorillas?

1   For almost 18 years, Dian Fossey lived among the mountain gorillas in central Africa. Little was known about these animals because they stay away from people. All Fossey knew was that if a way to protect them wasn't found, they would soon die out. To study them, this American woman acted like a gorilla. She pounded her chest with her fists. She scratched her head. She pretended to eat vines. And she made gorilla sounds. Finally, the gorillas got used to her. One day, Fossey crawled among a group that was feeding. While pretending to eat, she made gorilla noises. And the gorillas answered her!

2   After three years in the rain forest, Fossey was getting ready to leave on a trip. In the middle of packing, she stopped to relax. A gorilla named Peanuts came out of the forest and sat beside her. Fossey's hand was resting on the grass. Peanuts reached out his hand and gently touched it. The gorilla had accepted Fossey as a friend.

3   Fossey learned that mountain gorillas are shy and gentle. They live in family groups of up to about 40 animals. The leader of the group is usually a silverback, an older male. The rest of the group is made up of younger males and females with their babies. The gorillas eat berries and other fruit; plant roots, shoots, and leaves; bark; and sometimes ants. An adult male can eat as much as 65 pounds of food a day. So, gorillas need a big territory to search for food.

4   Fossey spoke all over the world about the plight of the gorillas. She also started a fund to find ways to help them survive. Besides loss of their lands and disease, the biggest threat to the gorillas is poachers. These people kill the animals to sell their body parts. Dian Fossey was murdered in her tent in the rain forest in 1985. Others now carry on her work to save the mountain gorilla.

Circle the correct answer for questions 1–5.
Write your answer to question 6 on a separate piece of paper.

1. The article does *not* tell _____.
   A how Fossey acted like a gorilla
   B how many gorillas Fossey studied
   C which gorilla Fossey held hands with
   D where Fossey lived among the gorillas

2. Which word in paragraph 4 means "a difficult or dangerous condition"?
   A loss
   B fund
   C plight
   D disease

3. Which paragraph tells how the mountain gorillas live?
   A 1
   B 2
   C 3
   D 4

4. Which of the following is *not* causing the gorilla population to decrease?
   A change in climate
   B loss of their lands
   C poachers
   D sickness

5. You can infer from the article that _____.
   A it can take a long time for gorillas to accept people
   B Fossey wanted to take some gorillas to a zoo
   C gorilla noises don't mean anything
   D Fossey liked eating vines

6. Today there are fewer than 600 mountain gorillas left in the world. Some people think that Dian Fossey's methods may be partly to blame. Do you think Fossey was right or wrong to let the gorillas become "friends"? Write your opinion and justify it with facts from the article and your own knowledge.

1 In Mexico, people celebrate a special holiday on November 1 and 2. It is called the Day of the Dead. Indians believe that on these days the souls of the dead return to where their bodies are buried. They come back to visit the living. So families cook a feast of their loved one's favorite foods. Then they go to the grave and cover it with flowers, candles, food, and drink. They wait quietly for the dead person to return.

2 At dawn on November 2, the families take the food and drink and go home. Now it's time for a party. The people eat and drink, sing and dance. In this way they respect the dead. But they also show that they're happy to be living.

3 The Day of the Dead is a very old holiday. It comes from Aztec times. Indians then did not fear death. In fact, they joked about it. To them, the skull was a promise of new life. The Aztecs used skulls to decorate many of their buildings and often hung one from a string around their necks.

4 Even today, Mexican Indians are not frightened by death. In songs it is "the thin one" or "the one with no hair." Sometimes death is "the one whose teeth always show." Children get used to it at an early age. They play with toys that represent death. On the Day of the Dead, people give presents of candy skulls or paper skeletons. They bake bread and cakes in the shape of bones. Real and paper flowers in yellow and orange hang everywhere. Those are believed to be the favorite colors of the dead. In Mexico, life and death go hand in hand on the Day of the Dead.

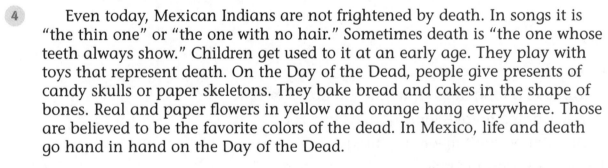

Circle the correct answer for questions 1–5.
Write your answer to question 6 on a separate piece of paper.

1. The Day of the Dead is _____.
   A not for children
   B an Aztec holiday
   C celebrated in Brazil
   D when Indians bury the dead

2. Which word in paragraph 4 means "be a sign or symbol of; stand for"?
   A represent
   B hang
   C play
   D give

3. Which paragraph tells how the Aztecs treated death?
   A 1
   B 2
   C 3
   D 4

4. You can infer from the article that most Mexicans _____.
   A are spiritual people
   B mourn death for many weeks
   C do not discuss death with their children
   D are no longer celebrating the Day of the Dead

5. *Grave* can have the following meanings. Mark the meaning used in paragraph 1.
   A serious
   B drab in color
   C low pitched in sound
   D hole in the ground for burial

6. How does the Mexican way of dealing with death compare with views of death in the United States? Which way to you think is better? Why?

1   The empty skyscraper stood on ground needed for a new train station. It was Jack Loizeaux's job to tear it down. But all around it were beautiful buildings. Could Jack get rid of the skyscraper without hurting them as well?

2   Many structures are knocked down by a swinging 4,000-pound ball. This can take months. The Loizeaux family tears down bridges, old hotels, and even ice jams on rivers in about ten seconds. Their tools are hundreds of pounds of dynamite, miles of wire, and weeks of careful planning.

3   Before the Loizeauxs tackled the skyscraper, they looked closely at the building plans. Jack decided which beams and columns supported the most weight. Then he and his sons drilled holes in them. Dynamite was placed in the holes. The most dangerous part came last. Jack had to be sure that the sticks of dynamite went off in a certain order.

4   Soon the dynamite and wires were all in place. The Loizeauxs looked over their work. Then Jack carefully looked at everything again. Finally he was ready. Jack flipped the switch. One after another, the blasts ripped through the 32 stories of the skyscraper. The ceiling and inside walls fell down first. Then the building's shell tumbled into the empty space at the center. In just eight seconds, the whole building had crashed into its own basement! Only a huge cloud of dust remained. And not a single window in nearby buildings was even cracked.

Circle the correct answer for questions 1–5.
Write your answer to question 6 on a separate piece of paper.

1. The skyscraper _____.
   A caught on fire
   B had no basement
   C was 32 stories high
   D fell on top of a nearby building

2. Which word in paragraph 3 means "set about dealing with"?
   A decided
   B tackled
   C drilled
   D placed

3. Which paragraph tells about the tools the Loizeauxs used?
   A 1
   B 2
   C 3
   D 4

4. Why were holes drilled in beams and columns?
   A to allow more air to pass through them
   B to allow workers to see through them
   C to hold balls of wire
   D to hold dynamite

5. You can infer from the article that _____.
   A Jack Loizeaux had one son and one daughter
   B the Loizeauxs built the new train station
   C the dynamite went off in the right order
   D the dynamite only works in skyscrapers

6. It takes special knowledge to tear down structures the way the Loizeaux family does. What do you think they have to know in order to do this work, and why?

1   In October 1998, a month before his 80th birthday, Earl Shaffer completed a remarkable journey. He walked out of a Maine forest after hiking the entire 2,150-mile Appalachian Trail. What's more, this was the third time he had made the trip. In 1948, Shaffer became the first solo "thru-hiker" of the trail. That meant he hiked continuously without leaving the trail for any length of time. In 1965, he made the journey again, beginning in Maine and finishing 99 days and 14 states later in Georgia. That made him the only person ever to have completed the hike in both directions.

2   The 1998 hike took Shaffer a little longer. He began in Georgia in May and finished 173 days later, the oldest person ever to hike the whole trail. For much of his journey, Shaffer had company. Hikers young enough to be his grandchildren would join up for a while. They liked being with him and listening to his stories. And Shaffer could spin yarns for every inch of the Appalachian Trail! He wrote hundreds of poems as well as a book about his first trip, *Walking with Spring*.

3   Shaffer was very well known because of the trail. So the hardest part of the 1998 hike was dealing with all the attention from the media. He preferred to be alone with the quiet of the trail. That way, he could appreciate the scream of a bald eagle as it soared by him on top of a mountain. Shaffer said that this hike was harder in another way, too. He didn't get to see much of the scenery. The trail seemed a lot rougher than before, so he had to watch his step. Still, he managed to hike about 12 miles each day.

4   The 1998 trip was Earl Shaffer's last thru-hike of the Appalachian Trail. Asked if he'd ever do it again, he quickly answered, "Absolutely not! I'm mighty glad it's over!"

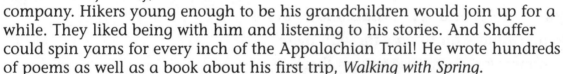

Circle the correct answer for questions 1–5.
Write your answer to question 6 on a separate piece of paper.

1. Earl Shaffer's second thru-hike took _____ days.
   A 12
   B 99
   C 173
   D 2,150

2. Which word in paragraph 3 means "beautiful view or landscape"?
   A trail
   B media
   C scenery
   D attention

3. Which paragraph tells about Earl Shaffer's second thru-hike of the Appalachian Trail?
   A 1
   B 2
   C 3
   D 4

4. What happened first in the life of Earl Shaffer?
   A He hiked the Appalachian Trail a month before turning 80.
   B He hiked the Appalachian Trail from Georgia to Maine.
   C He hiked the Appalachian Trail from Maine to Georgia.
   D He hiked the Appalachian Trail in 173 days.

5. You can infer from the article that _____.
   A Earl Shaffer's feet were sore after the hike
   B Earl Shaffer enjoyed telling stories of the trail
   C Earl Shaffer had only hiked the Appalachian Trail
   D Earl Shaffer is the only man who ever did a thru-hike of the Appalachian Trail

6. Using clues in the article and "reading between the lines," describe what kind of person you think Earl Shaffer was. Write a short character study of him.

Is there anywhere you will *not* find a spider?

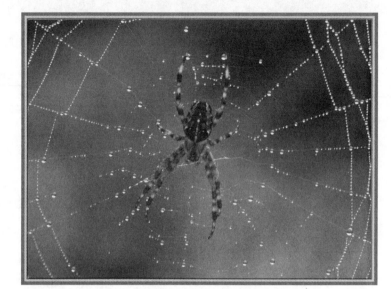

1   When a New York City family returned from a short vacation, they found their apartment the same as they had left it, except for one thing. In one of the closets was a spider web. Of course, it's not strange to find a spider web in a closet. But this family lived on the 30th floor!

2   Spiders are found almost everywhere in the world. They have been seen 22,000 feet up on Mount Everest. Sailors have even sighted them far out at sea, drifting with the wind on silken threads. And their numbers are incredible. Scientists believe that there are at least 50,000 spiders on every acre of country land. Each year these spiders eat a hundred times their number in harmful bugs.

3   There are many kinds of spiders. They can be as small as the head of a pin. Or they may be as large as a dinner plate. The world's largest spiders are tarantulas. Their bodies are thicker than a person's thumb. Some tarantulas have a leg spread of nearly 10 inches. Tarantulas often "star" in horror movies, but they just look ugly. Their bite is not nearly as dangerous as the black widow spider's. The poison of a black widow is stronger than a rattlesnake's. It causes intense pain. People can even die from this spider's bite.

4   One of the strangest spiders is the fishing spider. It can run across water, or it can stay under the water for as long as an hour. Coming to the surface again is no problem. The fishing spider holds a bubble of air under its body and just floats up!

Circle the correct answer for questions 1–5.
Write your answer to question 6 on a separate piece of paper.

1. Fishing spiders float upward on a _____.
   A bubble
   B thread
   C fish
   D web

2. Which word in paragraph 3 means "very great"?
   A horror
   B thicker
   C intense
   D stronger

3. Which paragraph tells about the sizes of spiders?
   A 1
   B 2
   C 3
   D 4

4. What is the main idea of the article?
   A There are many kinds of spiders.
   B Some spiders have a dangerous bite.
   C The fishing spider is one of the strangest spiders.
   D Spiders are found almost everywhere in the world.

5. You can infer from the article that _____.
   A a black widow spider's bite doesn't hurt
   B spiders are not found underground
   C spiders are helpful to farmers
   D fishing spiders eat fish

6. Write a letter to the editor of your local newspaper to persuade people not to kill spiders in their homes. Highlight the helpful things that spiders can do.

What is the "Chunnel"?

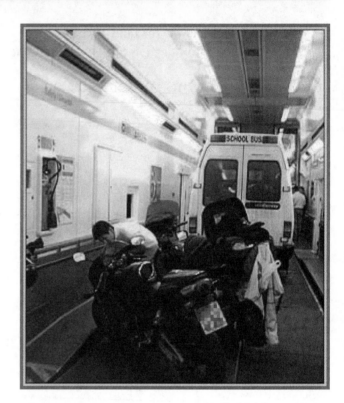

1   In the mid-1800s, Britain's Queen Victoria heard a new idea. It was to build a tunnel under the English Channel. This would connect the island nation with France. "What a good idea," said the queen. "All the ladies of England will be pleased." What Victoria meant was that the rough channel waters would no longer make people seasick!

2   Yet it wasn't until 1985 that Britain and France actually decided to go ahead with the tunnel. In 1987, work began on the English Channel Tunnel, or "Chunnel," from the British side. Early the next year, France began digging from its end. The idea was to build two tunnels for trains. A third tunnel in the middle would be used for repairs or emergencies. Cross passages would connect the three tunnels.

3   Machines called moles dug the tunnels. These monsters chewed through about 100 feet of rock each day. In front, the moles had a huge round head fitted with a metal pick and cutting disks. As the head slowly turned, the pick and disks ground through the rock and pushed it onto a belt. The belt carried the rock to rail cars that took it away. Behind the moles, workers lined the tunnel with concrete or metal.

4   The digging stayed on course with the help of laser beams. The beams hit a certain spot on the back of the mole. Other machines then noted if the mole needed to change course. In mid-1991, British and French workers at last met in the middle of the 31-mile Chunnel. Even though 23 miles were under 150 feet of water, the two rail tunnels met perfectly. The repair tunnel was off by only 4 inches one way and 18 inches the other!

Circle the correct answer for questions 1–5.
Write your answer to question 6 on a separate piece of paper.

1. The Chunnel _____.
    A opened to travel in 1991
    B was paid for by France
    C was built in 1985
    D is 31 miles long

2. Which word in paragraph 3 means "building material made of pebbles, sand, water, and paste"?
    A concrete
    B metal
    C mole
    D rock

3. Which paragraph tells how the tunnels met in the middle of the channel?
    A 1
    B 2
    C 3
    D 4

4. What happened last in the article?
    A Queen Victoria heard about the Chunnel.
    B Work began on the Chunnel from the British side.
    C Britain and France decided to go ahead with the Chunnel.
    D British and French workers met in the middle of the Chunnel.

5. You can conclude from the article that the Chunnel _____.
    A never would have been built without Queen Victoria
    B is a fast way to travel between England and France
    C has never been used for travel
    D starts under the city of Paris

6. It is said that technology has made the world smaller. Do you agree or disagree? Use the Chunnel to support your opinion.

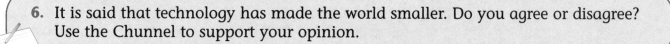

1 What animal has a call that sounds like a bugle playing "Taps"? It's the whooping crane. The "whooper" is the tallest bird in North America. It stands five feet tall, and its wings spread about eight feet.

2 When whooping cranes get ready to choose a mate, they do a dance that is beautiful to watch. The male and the female circle each other. They open their wings and bow their heads. Then they leap into the air. Whoopers mate for life. But if one of a pair dies, the survivor will seek a new mate. Sadly, though, there are far fewer whooping cranes dancing now than in the past.

3 Whooping cranes build nests in Wood Buffalo National Park in Canada's Northwest Territories. Each year, they fly over 2,500 miles south to winter in Texas. The birds used to stop and rest all along their flight path through the plains of the United States and Canada. But as people settled the land, their habitats were disturbed. Hunting, egg collecting, chemicals, and, most of all, collisions with power lines killed large numbers of birds. In 1954, there was just one flock of whooping cranes left. It had only 21 birds.

4 Today, laws protect whooping cranes and the lands they use. Scientists are working to save them in other ways, too. Captive breeding programs have been started in both the U.S. and Canada. If successful, these birds will help to rebuild the flocks in the wild. In fact, there is new hope for the whooping crane. Recent estimates suggest that there are more than 330 whooping cranes living in the wild, and another 130 or so living in captivity.

Circle the correct answer for questions 1–5.
Write your answer to question 6 on a separate piece of paper.

1. Whooping cranes nest in _____.
   A Texas
   B Mexico
   C Alaska
   D Canada

2. Which word in paragraph 4 means "kept within bounds; not free"?
   A breeding
   B rebuild
   C captive
   D started

3. Which paragraph tells about the size of whooping cranes?
   A 1
   B 2
   C 3
   D 4

4. Which was *not* one of the causes of the decreased whooping crane population?
   A hunting
   B chemicals
   C power lines
   D captive breeding

5. You can conclude from the article that whooping cranes _____.
   A reproduce frequently
   B haven't been studied
   C are difficult to preserve
   D would rather not migrate

6. Use information from the article and maps to describe the route whooping cranes might take to fly south.

1   The boy quietly watched the artist. The painting was taking shape right before his eyes. It was beautiful. Henry Ossawa Tanner decided then and there that he, too, would become an artist. For a young African American in 1872, though, that was no easy task.

2   Henry Tanner was serious about his art. He drew all the everyday places and people he knew in Pittsburgh, Pennsylvania. In the 1880s he studied at the Pennsylvania Academy of Fine Arts. Then Tanner went to Atlanta, Georgia, to teach at Clark University. He kept studying and painting what he saw around him. His early works show a very real feeling for the life of African Americans in the South. A famous picture from this period is *The Banjo Lesson.* In it, a little boy sits on the lap of an old black man. The man is teaching the child to play the banjo. Looking at the painting, you feel the love between the two.

3   Yet Tanner soon found that he'd learned all he could in America. Like many other American artists, he wanted to study in Europe. So Tanner left for Rome. But once he saw Paris, he couldn't leave. Paris, the City of Light, is a friendly place to artists.

4   After five years in Paris, Henry Tanner developed the style for which he is known. He began to use warm, rich colors. There were sharp differences between light areas and dark ones. For subjects, Tanner drew from his background as a minister's son. His new paintings were of stories from the Bible. In 1897 the French government bought one of them, *The Resurrection of Lazarus.* Soon, he began to win art prizes in both Europe and the United States.

Circle the correct answer for questions 1–5.
Write your answer to question 6 on a separate piece of paper.

1. Henry Ossawa Tanner went to Europe to _____.
   A hike the mountains
   B become a doctor
   C see the sights
   D study art

2. Which word in paragraph 4 means "a special way of doing something"?
   A style
   B differences
   C background
   D government

3. Which paragraph tells about Henry Tanner's early painting style?
   A 1
   B 2
   C 3
   D 4

4. What happened first in the life of Henry Tanner?
   A He left for Rome.
   B He lived in Paris.
   C He painted *The Banjo Lesson.*
   D He painted *The Resurrection of Lazarus.*

5. *Period* can have the following meanings. Mark the meaning used in paragraph 2.
   A completion of a cycle
   B punctuation mark
   C stage of culture
   D portion of time

6. Imagine that you are a young painter who goes to Europe to study art. What cities would you visit? What type of art would you create?

What is so special about Japanese gardens?

1   A Japanese garden puts you in harmony with nature. And that's what it's supposed to do. The world's first gardening book was written by a Japanese man about 1,000 years ago. He wrote that trees and plants bring the beauty of heaven down to earth. Japanese gardeners copy nature in order to make it better. So Japanese gardens are unique in all the world. Every rock, every plant, every tree is placed just so. Each part of the garden adds to the beauty of the whole.

2   There are many kinds of Japanese gardens. Some don't even have plants! They are made of boulders set in smaller stones. Some large rocks sit by themselves, others in groups. The smaller stones are raked into a pattern that "flows" like water from rock to rock. In fact, workers rake them every day so that the pattern never changes. They also make sure the garden stays "clean." Leaves or twigs that blow in are carefully picked up.

3   Most Japanese live crowded into big cities. They have little or no land of their own. So they use whatever they have. In gardening, this is called *shakkei,* or borrowed view. The gardener looks at what lies beyond the garden walls. Maybe there's a distant mountain. Tall buildings or low hills might be nearby. Whatever is there blends into the garden plan. It becomes part of the view.

4   For many years, the Japanese have followed three main belief systems—Taoism, Buddhism, and Shinto. Each in its way teaches people to live in harmony with nature. This idea finds its way into Japanese gardens. In them, busy people can slow down for a minute to just enjoy nature.

Circle the correct answer for questions 1–5.
Write your answer to question 6 on a separate piece of paper.

1. The Japanese _____.
   A all have their own gardens
   B don't take care of their gardens
   C try to copy nature in their gardens
   D like rocks better than plants in gardens

2. Which word in paragraph 3 means "taken and used as one's own"?
   A garden
   B distant
   C crowded
   D borrowed

3. Which paragraph tells about the first gardening book?
   A 1
   B 2
   C 3
   D 4

4. Why do some Japanese have a garden that is a "borrowed view"?
   A They are too busy to maintain a large garden.
   B They share the garden with a neighbor.
   C They do not have access to plants.
   D They have little land of their own.

5. You can infer from the article that Japanese people _____.
   A have no religion
   B have large houses
   C don't like gardening
   D find peace in their gardens

6. What do Japanese gardens tell you about the people of Japan? What do you think is important to them?

1   Two days are especially important in the lives of Korean children. They are *Paekil* and *Tol.* *Paekil* is the celebration of a baby's 100th day. *Tol* is the child's first birthday. To understand why these days are so important, you'd have to go back hundreds of years. At that time, many children didn't live to see their first birthday. So reaching the 100th day was a sign that the baby was healthy and would live.

2   Koreans still consider these days special. For *Paekil,* a big dinner is prepared. There are many different dishes for guests to enjoy. The baby's parents also give them rice cakes. Sharing food is believed to bring the baby a long and happy life. The guests in turn bring gifts of gold rings for the baby.

3   The *Tol* celebration is even bigger. For it, the child wears the *hanbok,* or Korean national costume. All the guests gather around the child. The child sits before a low table. On it are different foods and other things like thread, books, brushes, and money. Everyone tries to make the child pick up something from the table. Koreans believe that whatever the child chooses shows what he or she will be in life. A pencil or book means the child will be wise—a teacher. Money or rice is a sign that the child will be rich. And thread signals a long life. After the child's future is "told," it's time for fun. Guests play with the child and give presents of money, clothes, or gold rings to the parents. Later birthdays aren't nearly as big as that first one. And the children can't even remember their special day!

Circle the correct answer for questions 1–5.
Write your answer to question 6 on a separate piece of paper.

1. The article does *not* tell about _____.
   A the hanbok
   B the child's gifts
   C the second birthday
   D the reason for *Paekil* and *Tol*

2. Which word in paragraph 3 means "clothing of a certain group or country"?
   A celebration
   B costume
   C thread
   D guests

3. What happens last in a *Tol* celebration?
   A Guests give presents.
   B The child sits at a low table.
   C Guests gather around the child.
   D The child picks up items from the table.

4. *Paekil* celebrates _____.
   A a baby's birth
   B a baby's health
   C a baby's family
   D a baby's first birthday

5. *Before* can have the following meanings. Mark the meaning used in paragraph 3.
   A in front of
   B in advance
   C at an earlier time
   D in a higher position than

6. How is *Tol* similar to an American child's birthday party? How is it different? Why do you think Americans don't celebrate holidays exactly like *Paekil* and *Tol?*

Reading for Comprehension 87

1   The South American hoatzin (WAHT•seen) is a "rare bird" in many ways. First of all, a baby hoatzin has two claws on each wing. They may be left over from the bird's prehistoric ancestors. Yet these claws still come in handy. The young hoatzin is often hatched in a nest on a low branch hanging out over a river. So it uses its wing claws to climb around the tree branches. Sometimes it falls into the water or dives in to escape from an enemy. Then the baby bird uses its claws to pull itself back up the tree trunk. As the young hoatzin grows older, though, it loses the claws.

2   The grown hoatzin also stands out from other birds. For one thing, it looks like a feather duster blowing in the wind. Most of its feathers are dark brown or dull yellow. Its small head is topped with a crest of untidy brown feathers. Each eye is circled by a patch of bright blue skin. And the eyes themselves are a bright red. Even with all those feathers, the hoatzin has a flying problem. Its feathers are attached loosely to its body. And its body isn't well balanced. So the poor hoatzin has to flap its wings a lot just to get off the ground.

3   The hoatzin is rare in one other way, too. It smells. It is often called the "stinkbird" or "stinking pheasant." The strong odor keeps the hoatzin safe from other animals and people.

Circle the correct answer for questions 1–5.
Write your answer to question 6 on a separate piece of paper.

1. The article does *not* tell about the _____ of the hoatzin.
   A odor
   B food
   C color
   D feathers

2. Which word in paragraph 1 means "existing in times before there was writing"?
   A rare
   B young
   C ancestors
   D prehistoric

3. Why does the hoatzin have flying problems?
   A Its head is heavy.
   B It has poor vision.
   C Its feathers are loose.
   D It has claws on each wing.

4. You can conclude from the article that hoatzins _____.
   A never fly
   B fear water
   C look a lot like other birds
   D have something in common with skunks

5. *Dull* can have the following meanings. Mark the meaning used in paragraph 2.
   A lacking brilliance or luster
   B lacking sharpness
   C slow in action
   D mentally slow

6. Write a one- or two-paragraph summary of the article you just read.

Who was Miles Davis?

1   In 2006, Miles Davis was honored by the Rock and Roll Hall of Fame. This surprised a lot of people. Davis was best known for playing jazz. As it turns out, though, his playing has had a great influence on many other styles of music.

2   Davis was born in 1926. While he was growing up in St. Louis, he learned to play trumpet and became a fan of jazz. He went to New York to study music and joined a band there in 1946. The band was led by Charlie Parker. Parker played a fast, complicated form of jazz called *bebop.* Davis liked to play more slowly, and created his own style that he called *cool* jazz.

3   In the 1950s and 1960s, Davis continued to change his style. In the process, he changed jazz itself many times. His most famous album, *Kind of Blue,* is considered one of the most important albums in jazz. It introduced another style called *modal* jazz.

4   In the late 1960s, Davis lost many old fans and gained a lot of new ones with yet another new style. It was called *fusion* and used electric instruments and rhythms that came from rock and roll. Many jazz fans did not approve of this, but a lot of rock fans loved it. Fusion became very popular in the 1970s and was a major influence on *jam rock,* which is popular today.

5   Miles Davis died in 1991, but he kept on changing until the end. With his final album, called *Doo-Bop,* he became one of the first people to combine jazz with rap. If there is a Rap Hall of Fame someday, it will probably honor Davis as well.

Circle the correct answer for questions 1–5.
Write your answer to question 6 on a separate piece of paper.

1. The article does *not* say that _____.
    A Miles Davis played fusion
    B Miles Davis played the trumpet
    C Miles Davis combined jazz and rap
    D Miles Davis played the electric guitar

2. Which word in paragraph 5 means "last"?
    A end
    B final
    C well
    D died

3. Which paragraph tells how Miles influenced rock music?
    A 1
    B 2
    C 3
    D 4

4. You can infer from the article that _____.
    A not everyone likes it when someone changes a style of music
    B everyone who performs rap music was influenced by jazz
    C Miles Davis also played country music
    D Charlie Parker was from St. Louis

5. *Form* can have the following meanings. Mark the meaning used in paragraph 2.
    A shape
    B mold
    C kind
    D paper

6. What is your favorite kind of music? What do you like about it?

1   One day, a scientist was out in the field collecting snakes. She spotted a copperhead slithering through the grass. Quickly the scientist stepped back. She checked on the noose she used to catch the snakes. Just then she saw five more copperheads only a few feet away. And near her boot was still another!

2   Copperheads are the kings of camouflage. They are very hard to spot. A copperhead is light brown in color. It has dark brown bands going around its body. These colors let it blend in easily with the dead leaves and sticks around it.

3   Copperheads are born with their camouflage. But the young snakes also have a bright yellow tail. This tail comes in very handy. The young copperhead twists its tail so that it looks like a juicy yellow bug. Eyeing what it thinks will make a fine dinner, a frog hops toward the tail. In seconds, the frog ends up as the snake's dinner instead!

4   Because the copperhead is poisonous, being able to hide so easily makes it really dangerous. Its bite is not as deadly as a rattlesnake's. Yet the bite of a copperhead can be very painful. The poison comes out through two hollow fangs at the top of the snake's mouth. When the copperhead makes its move to bite, these fangs spring forward like an arrow shot from a bow. So when you go out into the woods for a walk, be sure to wear boots. Keep your eyes open and watch where you put your hands and feet.

Circle the correct answer for questions 1–5.
Write your answer to question 6 on a separate piece of paper.

1. Copperheads' colors let them blend in easily with _____.
   A all rocks
   B green leaves
   C frogs and bugs
   D dead leaves and sticks

2. Which word in paragraph 1 means "slipping and sliding"?
   A slithering
   B collecting
   C noose
   D catch

3. Which paragraph tells about the bite of the copperhead?
   A 1
   B 2
   C 3
   D 4

4. Why does a young copperhead have a bright yellow tail?
   A to attract frogs
   B to attract a mate
   C to stand out to humans
   D to stand out from other snakes

5. You can infer from the article that copperheads _____.
   A are found in caves
   B hide in the tops of trees
   C are likely to bite a person's feet
   D can blend in with any environment

6. Can you think of another animal that has good camouflage? Describe the animal and then compare it to the copperhead.

1   In 2003, the Nobel Peace Prize was given to a woman named Shirin Ebadi. Her name was not known to most people in the United States. In fact, she lives in a country that Americans cannot visit. The country is Iran.

2   Ebadi was born in 1947. In 1969, she earned a law degree. Later, she became Iran's first female judge. After the Islamic Revolution in 1979, though, women lost many rights. Because she was not a man, Ebadi could no longer be a judge. When she was offered a lesser job, she quit in protest. After this, she could not even renew her law license.

3   Ebadi could not practice law again until 1992. Despite that, she kept busy writing books about the law. Then, in 1992, she became active in the courtroom again. Since then, she has stood up for women, children, and others who have been denied rights in Iran. She has worked hard to change laws that forbid women to divorce or inherit property and has tried to protect children from abuse.

4   It is not surprising that Ebadi's work has not made her popular with many of Iran's leaders. She has been arrested a number of times, and some leaders of Iran spoke out against her Nobel Prize. Despite this, she continues to practice law, write, and teach. She has said that she hopes her Nobel Prize will inspire others to have courage and stand up for freedom.

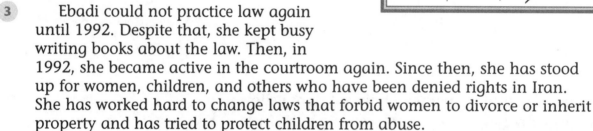

Circle the correct answer for questions 1–5.
Write your answer to question 6 on a separate piece of paper.

1. Shirin Ebadi could no longer be a judge because she _____.

    A was arrested

    B was not a man

    C was offered a lesser job

    D was busy writing books

2. Which word in paragraph 3 means "do not allow"?

    A protect

    B inherit

    C forbid

    D abuse

3. Which paragraph tells what Shirin Ebadi did after she lost her law license?

    A 1

    B 2

    C 3

    D 4

4. Shirin Ebadi has gotten in trouble in Iran mainly because she _____.

    A opposed Iranian laws

    B inherited a lot of property

    C was unemployed for a long time

    D supported the Islamic Revolution

5. You can conclude from the article that _____.

    A the revolution in Iran made it easier for women to get good jobs

    B there were many female judges in Iran before Shirin

    C Shirin Ebadi regrets causing so much trouble

    D Shirin Ebadi does not get discouraged easily

6. What is the Nobel Peace Prize? Use an encyclopedia or other reference to write one or two paragraphs about the prize.